# HOW TO HAVE

# REAL

# Conversation

# WITH YOUR TEEN

*Tips for parents from veteran youth workers —
with teens of their own!*

## Ron Habermas and David Olshine

STANDARD
PUBLISHING

Cincinnati, Ohio

All Scripture quotations, unless otherwise indicated, are taken
from the HOLY BIBLE, NEW INTERNATIONAL VERSION®. NIV®.
Copyright © 1973, 1978, 1984 by International Bible Society.
Used by permission of Zondervan Publishing House. All rights reserved.

Cover design by Matt Key
Interior design by Dana Boll

The Standard Publishing Company, Cincinnati, Ohio
A division of Standex International Corporation

05  04  03  02  01  00  99  98                                    5  4  3  2  1

Library of Congress Catalog Card Number 97-068978
ISBN 0-7847-0720-0

## From Ron

*To my faithful wife, Mary, and my three daughters,*
*Elizabeth, Melissa, and Susan.*
*Fred MacMurray of the TV show "My Three Sons"*
*never had it so good!*
*To our contributing authors for their fine work.*
*A huge thanks!*

## From David

*To Rhonda and Rachel for your gift of encouragement.*
*You are better than I deserve!*
*To Connie Wolfe, Dale Reeves, and Laura Ring*
*for their tremendous editing skills. Thanks.*

# Contents

## Real Faith

# What's this book about?

We couldn't find many books that really helped conversation work
between parents and teens, so . . . we wrote one! We hope this book
won't collect dust on your bookshelves. It's meant to be practical. Our
goal is simple: to help you communicate better with your teenage child.
To meet that goal we have included

- Ideas about what to say to your teen and how to say it
- Dialogues that get you thinking about family struggles
- Questions and illustrations to help you evaluate the messages you and
    your teen are sending to each other

   This book is divided into two parts. The first part is an in-depth look
at Relational styles in families, Empathizing with your teens, Active
Communication strategies, and how to use God's guidance to send Life-
changing messages—in other words, how to have **REAL** conversation
with your teens.

   Accompanying each of these chapters is a guide for either personal or
group study. If you use it alone, take your time. You may want to read
through the whole book first and then go back and concentrate on the
study sessions. Try to involve your spouse or close friends. They may be
able to help you look objectively at the communication patterns in your
family. If you're working with a group, the guides include outlines to help
you plan for four study sessions. The sessions could also be expanded if
your group would like to spend more time on a particular subject. No matter how you use them, we hope the questions and suggestions provided in
the study guides will help you break through the communication barriers
that may exist between you and your child.

   The second part of the book is a collection of anecdotes, advice, and affirmations that provides some fresh ideas, helpful reminders, and discussion topics for communication bridge building.

If you want to improve understanding between you and your kids, taking a closer look at the following four areas will help.

### Relational Styles

Before analyzing your communication habits, look at how you relate to your family members. Realize that the relationships between family members have a great effect on how you communicate with each other. And the way you relate today may be a result of the way your parents related to you! As the parent of a teenager (or a preteen, called a "tweenager"), recognize your strengths and your weaknesses. Be willing to look honestly at yourself and your family. Discover the patterns that may exist and see what needs to be changed.

### Empathizing With Teens

Treat each kid as an individual. Why? Because we cannot rubber-stamp teenagers into one "type." There is not just one way to parent, because there is not just one type of kid. Teens want to be accepted and understood. Learn to read them by trying to put yourself in their shoes, feeling what they feel. They express themselves in many different ways. Don't compare. Accept each one as a unique, God-given gift.

### Active Communication

Active communication doesn't mean that you get to do all the talking. Many times the things we say or the way we say them closes the door to communication before we even know what happened. Listen to yourself. Then listen to the reaction from your teen. Is there a certain pattern to your communication? Notice what gets a response and what doesn't. Later in the book you will find more questions and suggestions to help you communicate, but the first step is just to listen.

### Life-Changing Messages

God is the ultimate parent. He should be—he created parents! He is also a great communicator. Ask him for guidance as you listen and talk to your teen. Read his Word. Talk to him. Our faith shapes our lives every day. Everything we say or do sends messages about what we believe. What kinds of messages are your teens receiving from you? Are you tuned in to what God is saying to you? We have provided some Bible verses to get you started. But God has much more to say to you than what's in this book. After all, he knows your situation better than anyone!

## Who's writing this book?

If you've read the other two books that we have coauthored, *Tag-Team Youth Ministry* and *Down But Not Out Parenting*, you already know that we are parents of teenage girls. Our experiences with them, combined with what we've learned through our years of youth ministry and teaching courses on youth, have shaped and inspired the ideas in this book.

We don't pretend to know everything—we're still learning! But we do know that we love teens and we're committed to helping others develop better family relationships.

In order to avoid some unnecessary confusion, the rest of the book is written using "I" rather than "I, David" or "I, Ron." However, if you're reading one of our stories and you're really curious about which author is speaking, here's the key: In Part One, David is speaking. In Part Two, if Elizabeth, Melissa, or Susan is mentioned, it's Ron speaking. If Rachel is mentioned, it's David's story.

Now that that's all cleared up, turn the page and get started!

# Part One

▼▼▼▼▼▼▼

# CHAPTER ONE

# Real Conversation Is Relational

The relationships we have with our families have more influence on us than any others. Parents especially carry the responsibility of making an impact on their children. If communication between you and your teen is going to improve, it has to start with you. Know yourself—and your family relationships. Who are you? What's your family like? How do you communicate?

As a youth pastor, I've been able to observe many different kinds of family relationships. For example, consider a girl named Sherry. Sherry attended our youth retreat and spent the entire weekend hearing about God's desire for her. On Saturday evening, she became a Christian. She was radiant. Glowing. Alive.

When our group returned to the church on Sunday, many parents were there to pick up their children. But not Sherry's. After an hour, an old pickup truck came barreling into the parking lot. Sherry's look of joy changed to one of disappointment—almost sadness. Sherry climbed into her dad's truck, stared straight ahead, and left in a cloud of dust.

Two weeks passed. Sherry hadn't come to any group meetings. I asked some students if they knew what was going on. "Sherry's parents won't let her come back to youth group anymore," they reported.

At that point, I began to understand that the group that influences teenagers the most isn't youth workers, pastors, or even other teens. It's us, their families.

That's why it's so important that we understand family systems. In their book *Shaking the Family Tree*, Bill Berman and Dale Doty define a family system as a "nuclear family group (husband, wife, children) and the past three to seven generations in the families of both the husband and wife. . . . Family systems theory [studies] the way a family functions by studying [its] structure: what roles each member plays within the system, and what rules govern how that family functions in day-to-day life" (1991, 16).

Family systems theory asserts that the whole is greater than the sum of the parts. Families consist of individuals who are interconnected and interrelated. When trying to communicate, it's extremely important to understand how these connections work. To do that, we first have to ask, What kinds of family systems do we have?

## Systems—open or closed?

There are a variety of systems in life. Our body is a system. The church is a system. The universe is a system. We even call the government—shutdowns and all—"the system." The system we're concerned with here is the family. Studying your family system, Berman and Doty write, "helps you determine where your beliefs about families originated, and can aid in creating a successful marriage and in rearing well-adjusted children" (1991, 16).

The first step in improving the way you communicate is determining whether your family system is open or closed. One of the most inspiring moments in my life was witnessing the birth of my daughter, Rachel. She was wrinkled, slimy, crying—but very much alive. Everything about her was turned up to ten. Full blast. A newborn is probably the purest example of an open system.

I've also worked as a chaplain in hospital cancer wards. Men and women in these terminal conditions deteriorate before your eyes—it's gut-wrenching. Nothing seems more tragic. Dying systems. Closed systems.

So how can you tell if your family system is living or dying, open or closed? Measure it against the five basic characteristics of an open, living family system.

### Order

Any business, church, or family that's working and running well has a structure. What happens to a church without policies, order, and organization? Death—if the needs of the congregation aren't addressed and met. The same is true for families. An open family system has organization. Members have certain roles and are aware of their responsibilities. Rules are clear and well-defined. Is your family in order or chaos?

## Purpose

One of the first tasks of a new company is generating a mission statement, bylaws, objectives, and goals. When a family has direction, vision, and mission, it's alive. But when there's no unified purpose or plan, families splinter. As Proverbs 29:18 says, "Where there is no revelation, the people cast off restraint."

What would a family mission statement look like? Well, that would depend on your family, of course. But it could be something like this:

> We, the Olshines, are united for the purpose of loving one another and serving God and, to that end, will do everything we can to encourage, educate, and support each other.

Or you could get really specific:

> We, the Olshines, united by God, in an effort to promote love and peace, promise always to take out the garbage when asked, to make our beds every morning, to do our work as cheerily as possible with only a few complaints now and then, not to call each other names, not to speak in whining or mean voices, to welcome any and all slumber parties to our home as long as they come no more than five times a year, and to honor God through worship, prayer, service, and obedience as long as we live.

What's your family's mission?

## Adaptability

One sign of a dying marriage is resistance to change. Consider the husband and wife who get lost while driving. "Do you realize we're lost?" the wife asks rhetorically. The more she complains, the faster her husband drives. Finally, he can't take it anymore and pulls off the road. "OK, we're lost," he admits. "But at least we're making great time."

That couple is a closed system—they are shutting down and turning off. Family members who admit mistakes and are willing to change directions—especially in tougher times than a bad road trip—are more likely to see light at the end of the tunnel and grow closer in the process.

### Openness to Feedback

Communication and trust are at the heart of an open family system. Organizations prosper when they promote feedback and constructive criticism. The same is true for families. When family members tell each other the truth and share their feelings, it indicates that the family's vital signs are strong and healthy.

### Ability to Resolve Conflict

Conflict is inevitable in any system simply because systems are composed of different, interconnected parts. When there's a breakdown in the system—in even one part—confusion and chaos often result. Dysfunctional families rarely resolve conflict. The members usually don't have the skills or coping mechanisms required to handle issues effectively. On the other hand, family members who trust each other try to resolve problems.

After looking at these five characteristics, what's the impression you have of your family? Is your family an open system? a closed system? somewhere in between? It's important to know where you're starting before you make any changes. Keep reading for more information about family systems.

## Five family systems

Determining your family's degree of openness will tell you a lot about its health. But it's also helpful to determine which *type* of family system is yours: rigid, chaotic, disengaged, enmeshed, or balanced. The first two—*rigid* and *chaotic*—concern adaptability: How well does your family respond to change? The next two—*disengaged* and *enmeshed*—focus more on attachments: Are relationships in your family too close or too distant? The last model—the *balanced* system—is what God desires for us.

Some popular movies will help us conceptualize these different family systems.

# The Rigid Family

The climax of *Dead Poets Society* occurs when a teenage boy who has discovered the joys of theater is confronted by his rigid father. The father is displeased with his son's "rebellion" and basically says, "You're not going to ruin your life. I'm withdrawing you from school and enrolling you in a military academy. You are going to Harvard, and you are going to be a doctor!" The atmosphere becomes so oppressive and judgmental that the boy has no strength left to battle his father. He can't cope any longer. Following their argument, the boy commits suicide.

## In a rigid home,

## one directive reigns supreme:

## Do what the leader says or suffer the consequences.

In a rigid home, there's usually one leader. The subordinates know the rules are tight, often legalistic—sometimes militaristic. Discipline is harsh and strict. The leader, a control freak who always has to be in charge, lays down one directive: Do what I say or suffer the consequences. Flexibility and adaptability are nonexistent. Resistance is futile, possibly even life-threatening.

Since loyalty to the head of the family is intense, kids comply. But they do so out of fear, not love. Rigid parents often make high demands in areas such as academics or athletics, raising the expectations so high that the kids are eventually driven to compulsive, addictive behaviors. Failure to meet parents' high expectations only produces depression and low self-esteem. As parents keep demanding, children try harder and harder to please them. But eventually they resent their parents' taxing, unrealistic burdens and shut down. The result? Communication breakdown. As in *Dead Poets Society*, the teen is so intimidated by his manipulative parent that he doesn't even try to discuss his hopes or dreams. He just gives up.

## The Chaotic Family

The chaotic family is the other end of the adaptability pendulum. Instead of too much leadership, the chaotic family system has little or no leadership. Family members might discuss problems, but there's confusion about how to solve them.

*Mrs. Doubtfire* offers a classic example of the chaotic family. Robin Williams (the dad) and Sally Field (the mom) are heading for a divorce. Williams's character doesn't know how to lead, and his children are confused about who's in charge—Mom, Dad, or no one.

A chaotic parent operates impulsively and disciplines children erratically. Boundaries in this family system are blurry, cyclical, and unwritten. Children often assume the parental role (called *parentification*), taking on responsibilities that are beyond their emotional and mental capabilities. They have to be both son and father, or both daughter and mother. Consider Skip, whose parents divorced when he was in junior high school. By the time Skip reached high school, he was going to school, working two part-time jobs, organizing the checkbook, and delegating household duties to his younger sister. He was only sixteen, but his mother looked to him to be a husband and a father. What a tragedy.

The chaotic family system can also spawn *infantilization*—when teens are "demoted" to the status of a small child. Parents don't treat them as young adults, but as infants.

## A chaotic parent operates impulsively and disciplines children erratically.

Chaotic families often have good intentions but not much follow-through. Teens from such families often conclude that decisions in their homes aren't made—they just happen all of a sudden. For example, a couple with adolescent kids become Christians. One evening, out of nowhere, the father says, "Starting tomorrow, we're going to have devotions." The kids respond, "What are devotions?" The family reads the Bible for three days and then quits.

In rigid families, communication is top-down, from parent to child with no chance of dialogue. In chaotic families, harmony is desired to the point that conflict is avoided at all costs. Communication is minimal. The feeling is, "Let's deal with it later." Often, family members know little about each other and at times couldn't care less.

## The Disengaged Family

*Ordinary People*, the 1980 Academy Award-winning film, focuses on a character (played by Timothy Hutton) who attempts suicide after his older brother drowns in a boating accident. Following the death, the family grows apart, showing signs of anger, blame, and denial. As is typical of many disengaged families, the family members lack emotional closeness and the teenage child exhibits behavioral problems. Most notable is the identified patient syndrome (IPS). The identified patient becomes the family scapegoat, unfairly bearing problems and consequences, and often rebelling through drugs, violence, and truancy. In *Ordinary People*, the teenager's IPS stems from blaming himself for his brother's death.

## The disengaged family hasn't bonded— its members lead disconnected lives and rarely communicate.

Disengaged families lack intimacy. Members seem independent and isolated. If a family member is asked, "Do you love each other?" the answer might be, "Sure. But we're so busy that we don't get much time together." To disengage means to separate, dissociate. The disengaged family hasn't bonded—its members lead disconnected lives and rarely communicate.

Can the disengaged family bond? Yes, but with great difficulty! There is little loyalty present and plenty of independence. Decisions are made individually. Dinners are rarely eaten together, and family members are constantly coming and going on different schedules. Usually there's little interaction in disengaged families.

# The Enmeshed Family

In *Only the Lonely*, John Candy plays a police officer who has lived with his mother all his life. Candy's character, now in his thirties, meets a woman (played by Ally Sheedy) and falls in love. On the night before their wedding, he envisions his mother getting killed in a car wreck on her way home from the rehearsal dinner. His fiancée rightfully wonders whether his behavior—calling his mother every five minutes—will last their entire marriage. He's enmeshed with his mother, continually lost in her world.

## Teens may use words and phrases such as "smothered" or "suffocating" when describing an enmeshed home.

The enmeshed family system exhibits unhealthy closeness. Teens may use words and phrases such as "smothered" or "suffocating" when describing their home lives. Parents may become so absorbed in the lives of their children that they ignore the condition of their marriage. They may be overprotective of their children or even jealous of other friends or activities that take up their children's time.

An enmeshed person is entangled in a web of relationships with no clear boundaries. Those outside this family system may assume an enmeshed family is really close. But insiders are probably thinking, Let me out of here!

# The Balanced Family

In *Father of the Bride*, there is laughter, camaraderie, hugging, forgiveness, and flexibility. George Banks (played by Steve Martin) learns unexpectedly that his only daughter, Annie, is engaged. He responds with a range of emotions—from denial to anger, to stubborn disapproval. Finally he develops a gentle, winsome attitude that allows Annie to spread her wings.

## The balanced family stands apart because of healthy interdependence.

You might be wondering if there are any balanced families! There are. In fact, even the four dysfunctional family systems can experience moments of wholeness. But the balanced family stands apart because of its healthy interdependence. It is a safe place where members learn the value of clearly defined boundaries. The rules are fair, understood, and consistent. This family system places a high priority on elastic leadership—pliability and adaptability. The roles are clear—moms are moms, dads are dads, and kids are kids. Dolores Curran describes a balanced family in her book, *Traits of a Healthy Family* (1983: 23, 24). The healthy family

1. Communicates and listens.
2. Affirms and supports one another.
3. Teaches respect for others.
4. Develops a sense of trust.
5. Has a sense of play and humor.
6. Exhibits a sense of shared responsibility.
7. Teaches a sense of right and wrong.
8. Has a strong sense of family in which rituals and traditions abound.
9. Has a balance of interaction and sharing.
10. Has a shared religious core.
11. Respects the privacy of others.
12. Values service to others.
13. Fosters table time and conversation.
14. Shares leisure time.
15. Admits to and seeks help with problems.

The members of a healthy, balanced family appreciate each other. Mutual respect is evident. Each member is encouraged to grow and develop. And because of the freedom to develop, parents and siblings talk and listen with great interest and excitement. Family members remain close but don't compromise their individuality. Bottom line: Members of a balanced family system can be autonomous without being isolated, and attached without being suppressed.

# For More Help

After thinking about these family systems, maybe you've come to the conclusion that your family of origin (the one in which you grew up) or your present family isn't the greatest. Don't lose hope. There are some steps you can take to improve your relationships.

*The first step is to uncover your family system's baggage.* Family habits and patterns do not emerge out of a vacuum. Chances are we are parenting as our grandparents and parents did. It's scary to think that our destructive patterns will be passed down to our kids and grandkids unless we wake up and smell the coffee. This does not mean we should blame previous generations. But it does mean we should become a student of history—our family history. Use the study session at the end of this chapter to help you learn more about yourself and your family.

*Another step you can take is to ask some peers for support.* Many groups for parents of teens are springing up all over the country. Some are support groups that share their hurts and joys and experience Christian community. Others are accountability groups that allow adults to care for each other through prayer and Bible study.

*There are many resources to help you be a better parent.* Remember, the Lone Ranger needed Tonto, Laurel needed Hardy, and Batman needed Robin. Take advantage of the many manuals, teaching tools, books, seminars, and conferences that are out there today. Be a learner. Allow mistakes to teach you new lessons.

Sometimes getting counseling is the one step many reject until the problems seem insurmountable. *But there are many quality professionals who can help you be a winner at home.* Resist the two extremes of parenting: "I am an awesome parent; I have little to learn" and "I am such a lousy person; I will never improve."

*Let friends speak boldly and confront you if necessary to help you improve the way you communicate with your spouse and kids.* Share the discovery process with your spouse. Do whatever it takes to build a healthy, balanced family. Serve and love God by making your family top priority—number one, superseding work and success.

You may find the support you need in a Sunday school class, a Bible study group, a circle of friends or a parent support group in your community. No matter what type of group it is, it's a good idea to have some trusted people to care for you. To pray for you. To help you take a closer look at yourself and your family.

# Study Session One

▼▼▼▼▼▼▼▼▼▼▼▼▼▼▼

Use the questions and activities below as a guide for your personal study. At the end of each study session there is an outline and more suggestions for how to use the study guide in a group setting.

## The main point

To explore your family background and discover your parenting style.

## Think it out

Picture yourself at age thirteen. At the top of a piece of paper, write: "When I grow up, I will always/never . . . "

Think of ways to finish this sentence (or remember all the ways you used to finish this sentence as a teen!). When you are finished with your list, it might be a good idea to share your answers with your spouse, your friend, or better yet, with your teen!

## Ask yourself

Use the **past** space to answer about what your family was like when you were growing up (you, your parents, and your siblings). Then, use the **present** space to answer concerning your family now (you, your spouse, and your children).

1. Who is in charge? That is, who makes the rules? Who enforces them? Who makes the major decisions?

   Past:


   Present:

2. Does each person have a specific "job" in the family structure? List the name of each person in your family with the job or role that corresponds to that person.

Past:

Present:

3. Are decisions that concern the whole family open for discussion? What is the response from parents when a child in your family voices opinions or ideas? How is criticism offered by parents?

Past:

Present:

4. How does your family handle change? Are family members open to changing their opinions? their schedules? Think about the toughest time that your family went through. How did each family member deal with the experience? How did they handle the changes?

Past:

Present:

5. What are the topics that are most likely to be the cause of conflict in your family? In other words, if you want to start a fight, all you have to do is mention . . .

Past:


Present:


6. Think about each of your family members. When there is an argument in your family or there is some kind of conflict, what do they do? How do they react? With anger? violence? silence? raised voices? bitterness? other?

Past:


Present:


7. Are conflicts resolved in your family? How are they resolved?

Past:


Present:

8. Think about the individuals in your family and how they interact. Consider their personalities, goals, dreams, and needs. Based on the interactions of your family now, write a statement describing your family. State your family's purpose for being together.

9. Now write a mission statement reflecting what you would like your family's purpose or vision to be. (Look at page 19 for an example of a family mission statement.) How is it different from what you wrote above?

10. Now, considering your answers and what you've read regarding family systems, look at the chart below. Do any of the characteristics in the chart correspond to your family? to your family of origin? Try to identify what family system type(s) best describes your family now and your family of origin.

## What's Your Type?

| PARENTING STYLE | DISPOSITION | OUTCOMES/REACTIONS |
|---|---|---|
| RIGID | ANGRY, PUSHY | TEENS FEEL INTIMIDATED, USED, BEAT UP |
| CHAOTIC | INCONSISTENT | TEENS FEEL DIRECTIONLESS, INSECURE |
| DISENGAGED | UNAVAILABLE, BUSY | LACK OF BONDING, UNITY, CLOSENESS |
| ENMESHED | WANTS TO KNOW EVERYONE'S BUSINESS | TEENS FEEL OVERWHELMED, EVEN CRITICIZED |
| BALANCED | FLEXIBLE, SENSITIVE, HUMOROUS, FORGIVING | KIDS FEEL RESPECTED AND LOVED |

**(OLSHINE 1996, 34)**

Look honestly at your family history. What past behaviors—negative and positive—have contributed to your attitudes and well-being? What fears, habits, patterns, and attitudes do you have? Do any of your relatives share these? Look into it. Take a family systems course at a local college, or read some books to help you see where you've been so you can heal the wounds you may be carrying. Remember that what we as parents reproduce in our children can be passed down by them to their children.

## Look it up

Read Ephesians 5:21-6:4.
Think about the roles of family members. Paul tells us to submit to one another. If everyone in your family followed this command, how would your family be different? How would your answers to questions 1–10 change?

## Do something

- Rent the movies mentioned in the family systems section and watch some clips of each one. Do you identify with a particular family or character? Watch them with your family members. Whom do they identify with?

- Get some old magazines and make a "family portrait." Cut out pictures, words, colors, articles, etc. that represent each member of your family and glue them on a large sheet of paper or poster board. As you glue the pieces on the paper, think about the relationships between the people. Position your pictures in a way that represents those relationships. (For example: you might put a pair of baby shoes and a mother figure close together, while an electric guitar, representing your teenage son, may be standing alone.)

- For further study, read some of the stories in the section entitled "Real Parents" (pp. 83-95). Do you identify with any of those situations? Write your own reflections on being a parent of a teenager.

## Lift it up

Close your study time with prayer, asking God to heal wounds from the past and prepare you for the changes needed now. Praise God for the good qualities of your family relationships. Search your heart for areas where forgiveness or healing is needed. Ask God to help you see ways in which to improve your ties with family members.

# For Group Study

## Start it up

Use the "Think it out" question to get discussion going in the group. Divide the class into groups of three or four. Provide the groups with paper and pens or pencils. Give all the groups about ten minutes to think of ways to finish the sentence, then come together and share answers.

## Talk it out

Read Ephesians 5:21-6:4 together (one person could read it aloud or take turns reading the verses). Remaining in small groups, discuss questions 1, 2, 4, 6, and 8 (these could be written on a board for all to see or typed up beforehand and handed out to each group). Remember to talk about the past and the present. At the end of discussing these questions, ask: How would your answers to these questions be different if all your family members followed the command to submit to one another? Have some members of your class or group share their reactions.

## Do something

Rent the movies or make "family portraits" as described in the "Do something" section on page 31.

## Lift it up

Close with prayer. Ask members to suggest areas where prayer is needed concerning their families or family relationships in general.

▼

# Just for fun

Here's an idea for an activity that could be done with a Sunday school class or for a special youth group or "family night" activity. Have a teen/parent or class scavenger hunt. Break into teams (if including teens, each family can be a team). Each team has thirty minutes (can be longer if you have more time) to complete the hunt. Be creative. Bring as many items as possible. The group must stay together and can only spend $5. To earn the points listed for each number, the team must get at least two of the items listed with that number (600 total possible points). The team with the most points wins!

1. Megaphone, microphone, or hearing aid (10)
2. Mattress, sawhorse, or back-scratcher (20)
3. "No Smoking Please" sign or flag (20)
4. Bridge, airplane, or parachute (80)
5. Frisbee, tennis racquet, football, or joke book (10)
6. Silverware, towels, soft drink can, or garbage can (10)
7. Bible, devotional book, or copy of the Ten Commandments (20)
8. Christmas tree, board game, or cards (30)
9. Telephone, "kid's meal," postcard, or letter (20)
10. Christian book, CD, tape, or video (40)
11. "Do Not Disturb" sign, "Beware of Dog" sign, or "Knock Before Entering" sign (60)
12. Rake, hoe, or apron (50)
13. Plate, cup, napkin, or place setting (40)
14. Jogging outfit, sports equipment, water skis, or lawn chair (70)
15. A life preserver, or a police officer (120)

When you get back together, go over each item. The above numbers correspond with those of the list from *Traits of a Healthy Family* on page 25. Have the teams discuss the areas in which they are strong or weak and what areas they want to work on more.

# CHAPTER TWO

# Real Conversation Is Empathetic

There once was a man who tried to invent a device that would make a lasting difference in the world. He tried his experiment a hundred times without success. Then two hundred times. Nothing. Three hundred, four hundred, five hundred times. Zilch. No go. Nothing worked. But the man kept at it. After over nine hundred attempts, finally it happened. A lightbulb had been created.

Thomas Edison. A man for his times. Over nine hundred times!

Edison said that every time he made a lightbulb that didn't work, he learned "one more way not to make a lightbulb." Because of his persistence, we have incandescent light. He never quit. He stayed with it until he found success.

Sounds like parenting teens, doesn't it? Do you ever feel like calling it quits? Probably more times than you are willing to admit. Withdrawing sounds more relaxing, less stressful. Communication is tough stuff. We try to produce a "quality" child, yet sometimes nothing seems to work. All the how-to techniques in the books and tapes sound great until we try to use them! Parenting teens requires stick-to-itiveness, persistence, and a commitment for the long haul. We get weary after a while.

Both teens and parents find it difficult to communicate with each other. In one of the few books on this subject, *The Friendship Factor*, Alan Loy McGinnis writes:

The fundamental complaint of young Americans . . . does not refer to the hypocrisies, lies, errors, blunders, and problems they have inherited. It is, instead, this: That they cannot talk with grown people. . . . I have come to believe that the great majority of our kids have never enjoyed an intimate friendship with even one grown person. Why not? When you ask that, you get one answer: Their efforts to communicate with us are invariably and completely squelched (1979, 113).

Part of the reason for this difficulty is that adults often forget what it's like to be a teenager. We either treat our teens like adults or we approach them as if they were aliens, or people with a strange illness.

Adolescence is not an illness or a disease (although Sigmund Freud thought it was close to mental illness!). Adolescence is a developmental stage. A season of life—and a long one at that! It is moving out of childhood into the adult world. This stage of growth is necessary, essential, and, get this—normal!

During adolescence, four developmental tasks occur. *First is autonomy.* Autonomy is a quest for independence. The teen begins to establish intellectual and emotional independence from her parents. It is almost a time of disengagement. Some psychologists call this individuation. The teen is learning to make decisions and choices on her own and wants to be a responsible adult (scary thought!). Do you remember when your kids were five years old and they hung on you like moss on a tree? Now at fifteen, they don't want to be seen with you at the mall!

*Second is the emergence of peer friendships.* As individuation takes place, peer friendships become more important than life itself. Friendships are the glue that holds many teens together. They select their social network by themselves and without our help!

*The third issue teens have to face is the changing of their bodies.* All of a sudden, puberty kicks in, hormones rage, and—Boom!—sexuality emerges. They come to terms with their changing bodies, their own sexual development, and yes, the opposite sex. Teens grow at irregular and jolting rates. Some research indicates that girls mature two to four times faster than boys, both physically and emotionally. In his book, *Ten Mistakes Parents Make With Teenagers (and How to Avoid Them)*, Jay Kesler writes about young teens going through these changes.

> Internally, however, these boys are feeling certain urges and interests, which they express clumsily by teasing the girls, hitting them, insulting them, or, in some instances of immature bravado, talking dirty. All this seems childish and disgusting to the girls who are

only interested in the ninth- and tenth-grade boys anyway. The girls aren't secure either, of course. Like kittens in a barnyard who do a figure eight around your legs, leaning all the time, teenage girls need lots of assurance. They need to lean even while they think they're standing on their own (1988, 7).

*Finally, teens are developing their life skills (vocation).* They are pondering job possibilities, their future, and the impact of education on their careers. As they do their household chores, summer jobs, part-time school jobs (even full-time work while in school), they are thinking about college or trade school, settling down someday, where they'll live, what they'll be doing, and how they will make a difference in the world. The chart on the next two pages shows some common characteristics of teenagers that reflect these four developmental tasks.

These radical changes in teens trigger waves of emotions. The primary feelings that come with the turbulent teen years are inferiority and self-doubt. This causes stress and confusion for both teens and parents. These feelings also cause language gaps and barriers. Communication takes off in new ways, sometimes in opposite directions. When a parent knows that these feelings are typical, the knowledge can reduce the anxiety so often associated with raising a teenager.

Another way to reduce anxiety is to realize that there is no perfect way to raise all teenagers. Every teen, every person, is different from others. Learn to recognize how your teen expresses himself.

Become a student of youth culture. Actually, *your* youth's culture! Learn to understand things from your teen's point of view. Get inside his territory. Watch the shows she watches, listen to the radio station he listens to. Try to get into your teen's world.

For example, learn when to give space and when to express affection. Is your child an introvert who needs some privacy to unwind and disengage from people? Is your adolescent an extrovert who wants to go out with friends all the time? Read your teens' rhythms and moods. Know their likes and dislikes: study how your kids discover life. Kids have their own styles of listening, talking, and learning.

Even teens of the same family can be completely different. For example, consider Emily and Ben. Emily is the firstborn child. She's your standard high achiever. Emily doesn't come home with grades lower than an A. Emily is a classic introvert, deriving pleasure from being alone. An inner-world thinker, she processes thoughts quietly and rarely exerts herself in dialogue with others. If you want a long conversation with her, well, forget it.

# Age Characteristics of Teens

| | 7th Grade | 8th Grade | 9th Grade |
|---|---|---|---|
| **EMOTIONAL** | Desire to be considered grown-up. Unstable feelings. | **Sensitive to anything that makes them seem different. Very unsure of self.** | In need of feeling of success by developing a special ability or all-around competence. |
| **INTELLECTUAL** | Security is enhanced by definite concrete learning material. Abstracts are difficult. | **Knowledge greater than experience; pressure to succeed in getting good grades.** | Interested in current events, war, social issues. Begin to think of special interests and future plans. |
| **SOCIAL** | Loyal to the codes of their peers. Would rather sacrifice adult approval than lose status with peers. Conform to the group. | **Girls more interested in boys than boys are in girls. Over-aggressive show-off behavior may be apparent in order to protect ego.** | More permanent friendships with few selected friends. Less concerned about their variations from the pack. Boys less mature. |
| **PHYSICAL** | Still difficult to sit for extended periods of time. Girls usually complete their growth spurt by the end of the 7th grade. Boys are far behind. | **Girls are taller and more developed than boys. Boys are growing but still smaller than girls.** | Girls and boys become more equal in development. Boys are finally taller than girls. Most have reached puberty. |
| **SPIRITUAL** | Need to take things one step at a time. Beginning to question and probe things that were once taken for granted. | **Very concerned about "what good will I get out of it?" Keen sense of justice and fair play.** | Capable and ready to make strong commitments. In effort to be independent, may reject established values. |

| 10th Grade | 11th Grade | 12 Grade |
|---|---|---|
| **Confused—at home they are old enough to take responsibility for chores, studies, etc., but still considered to be children.** | Idealistic. May become disillusioned about conditions they observe in society. | **Relatively stable in feelings and attitudes. Sophisticated young adults in one situation and frightened youth in another.** |
| **Capable of formal thought. Can deal with abstracts. More complex thinkers.** | Ability to think critically begins to develop. | **Capable of thinking abstractly. Question things formerly taken at face value.** |
| **Strong desire to be accepted. Begin to "go steady" for date assurance. At the "crush" stage.** | Begin to break away from the gang. May start part-time jobs. Friendships are more permanent. Cliques often develop. | **Confident in front of groups. Concerned with "who else is doing it?" Very interested in the opposite sex.** |
| **Boys grow rapidly. Appear listless and lazy.** | Girls have stabilized. Boys are still growing. | **Boys and girls quite mature (basically equals).** |
| **Begin to establish personal value system.** | Will state convictions regardless if they differ from the crowd. | **Handle principles and concepts well.** |

Emily's younger brother, Ben, is the opposite of her. He's a classic extrovert, thriving on being with other people. Emily is pooped by a party. Ben's a party animal. Ben loves people. Emily enjoys cuddling up with a good book. Same family. Same parents. Different ways of responding.

Take a look at a few more different styles of teen expression.

- Anthony is an analytical learner who thinks deeply about everything. He uses his head. He is a whiz kid who likes data and facts and is fairly skeptical. Analytical learners tend to like computers and anything auditory and complex. What is amazing about analytical learners is they do listen to "smart" adults on occasion.

- Bonnie is a big-picture thinker who sees the forest but runs into the trees. She has a vision for her youth group and her school. She wants her friends to become Christians and involve themselves in work projects. She has dreams for the future but can't seem to clean up her bedroom!

- Elizabeth is a detail learner who sees short-term goals but does not think long-term. Liz can take a complicated and detailed problem and break it down into manageable and practical parts. But when you ask Liz to share her plans for her future, she shrugs and replies, "I dunno." She lives in the present, not the future. So do most detail learners.

- Ryan is a visual learner. He needs word pictures to bring things to life. Visual learners learn best when they gain insight by using a vivid picture or image. They love to read and enjoy anything visual.

- "Talk as they think" teens process their thoughts as they are talking. These auditory-oriented teens just need a pair of ears to hear them (even if the only ears available are their own). Some are process learners and enjoy discussing issues and raising questions. Your inquisitive teens may learn best by dialogue and hearing others' ideas.

- Adventure teens love action and discover by doing, not by listening. Matthew is a dynamic learner. He has trouble taking notes in class and struggles with sitting still. Students like Matt love to experiment with fun activities, rope courses, retreats, or sports.

It also may be helpful to realize what you and your teen have in common with each other. Parents with teens today struggle with their own issues. How do our midlife issues compare with our teens' developmental tasks?

- Teens are searching for some independence. So are we!
- Teens are trying to figure out what they want to do with their lives. Yes, we are too.
- Teens are stressed out. We are great worriers.
- Teens are somewhat fearful about the future. What about you? Is your company downsizing? How is your 401(k) going to last through retirement?
- Teens wonder if they can make an impact in the world. We are asking the same question.
- Teens think about sex. Parents think about—well, yes sirree!

We all have pressures to face and options to figure out. Kids are trying to figure out whom to date. Parents are remembering their own poor dating choices (some of them with lifelong consequences). Kids are uptight about classes. Parents are stressed over work. Teens are concerned about relationships. Parents are concerned about their own parents aging and their own mortality. Raising teens has been called adolescence all over again. And in the same household, when puberty hits at the same time midlife stresses peak, it's a double whammy! Expect some tension, but also realize that you can learn from each other. Remember what it's like to be in a teen's shoes.

# Study Session Two

Parents who lose touch with memory lane will probably lose touch with their teens. Even though times have changed ("We were never their age," one priest commented.), as teens, our attitudes, communication patterns, and habits were quite similar to those of our kids. The only things that have really changed are the options and choices our culture throws at our teenagers.

The adolescent years are turbulent. It will help if we can reflect on the way things used to be, and the way we used to be (rebellious? bossy? rowdy? hardheaded?). It can forge a common bond between us and our kids and give us things to talk about! For example, my daughter dies of laughter every time I show her pictures of my long hair in high school!

## The main point

To be able to empathize with your teen by seeing the world from a teen's point of view and to recognize the areas in which you need to improve your understanding of your teen.

## Think it out

Remember when you were fifteen years old. Think about what you did and how you felt. Answer these questions for yourself.

1. What were your biggest complaints about your parent(s) when you
   were a teen?
   a. don't trust me
   b. out of touch
   c. uncool
   d. boring
   e. legalistic
   f. domineering
   g. know-it-all
   h. never around
   i. bad listeners
   j. other_____

2. What subjects were you able to discuss freely with your parent(s)?
   a. friends
   b. sports
   c. opposite sex
   d. school
   e. drugs
   f. music
   g. very little
   h. movies/TV
   i. Christianity
   j. none of the above
   k. other_____

3. When I shared something important with my parent(s), they
   normally
   a. read the newspaper
   b. gave me full eye contact and listened with interest
   c. told me not to worry about it
   d. gave me the "When I was your age" lecture
   e. rolled their eyes
   f. rarely looked at me
   g. said "huh" after I was done
   h. other_____

4. On a scale of 1 to 10 (1=really bad, 10=super intimate), when you tried to communicate with your parent(s), how did you do?

   1    2    3    4    5    6    7    8    9    10

5. What was your favorite TV show? Hottest movie of the year? (Or only movie of the year!)

6. Where did you hang out?

7. What type of music did you listen to?

8. What kind of people did you associate with?

9. What kind of clothes did you wear?

10. What was the number one fad when you were fifteen?

# Ask yourself

Now it's time to come back to the present. Think about your own preteen or teenager. What do you know about him or her? Don't panic if you don't know all the answers. But do accept the challenge of finding out more about your teen.

1. Is he a morning person? An evening person? What time is the best for you to talk with your teen?

2. What is your teen's favorite type of music? TV show? Movie? Why?

3. What are some of your teen's pet peeves? What really drives her crazy?

4. What are your teen's biggest fears?

5. What are your teen's biggest dreams?

6. Who does your teen like to hang out with? Where do they like to go?

7. What are your teen's favorite subjects in school? Worst subjects?

8. Who does your teen want to be like? Why?

9. What are the biggest problems your teen has emotionally, intellectually, socially, physically, and spiritually?

10. What are your teen's best qualities?

Again, don't feel like a rotten parent if you don't know everything about teen culture today. After all, we are parents. We're supposed to be a little clueless. If we weren't, our teens would have nothing to complain about when they talk with their friends! But it is important to know about your teen's culture.

So how do you go about finding the answers? Well, don't grab the detective gear and start spying on your teen. And don't put your teenager under a bright light and give her an inquisition. Just relax and keep reading. The next chapter tells about some communication styles that just might be the way to solving the mystery of your teen's life.

# Look it up

Read 1 Timothy 4:7-16. Think about these questions.

1. What kinds of myths exist about teens today? What are the stereotypes? What do you think a godly view of teens might be?

2. Where do you place your hope? Do your teens have the same hope? How can we show them the hope in the living God?

3. Read 1 Timothy 4:12. What lessons can you learn about speech from teens? about living life? about love? about faith? about purity? What lessons are they learning from you?

4. The end of 1 Timothy 4 tells us to be diligent and watch our lives. But notice that Paul says to do this so that others can see your progress. You don't have to turn into a perfect parent all at once. Living a godly life is a process. Your children need to see what being a Christian is really about—not some phony image. How can you involve your children in this process?

## Do something

- "Draw" a word portrait of your teen. As you think of each feature of his face, write at least one good quality in the appropriate position on the picture (for example, eyes: he sees everyone as equals). This would also be a great activity to do with your teen. Let her draw a picture of you!

- Role-play a conversation between a parent and a teen. You could do this with your spouse or with your teen. You could play your teen and your teen could play you. Use one of the ideas from the topics in the section entitled "Real Teens" (pp. 97–121) to get your conversation going. Make sure that you really stay in character! If you want, switch roles (you could play one of your teenager's friends) and choose a different topic.

## Lift it up

Close your personal time with prayer. Lift your teen up to God.

# For Group Study

## Start it up

Divide into groups of three or four and use the "Think it out" questions to start discussion.

## Talk it out

Before your class or group meeting, type questions 1-10 from the "Ask yourself" section on a sheet of paper. Make enough copies for everyone in the group. During class, pass these sheets out and allow time for all members to complete their answers.

Divide into groups of three or four. Have someone in each group read 1 Timothy 4:7-16. Lead the group in discussing questions 1-4 from the "Look it up" section.

## Do something

- Role-play as described. Let half the group be teenagers and half be the parents. After the debate/discussion/argument is finished, talk about how you felt as you played the parent or teenager in this situation.

- Invite a panel of teenagers to your class. Have members of your class write questions on pieces of paper beforehand. The questions should be related to what it's like to be a teenager today. Conduct the class like a talk show—teens are the expert guests, parents are the audience.

## Lift it up

Close the class in prayer. Suggest that each person say at least a sentence or two about their teenager(s), lifting them up to God's care.

# CHAPTER THREE

# Real Conversation Is Active

Stop talking! OK, so maybe that seems like a strange way to begin a section on active communication, but I still think it's a good idea. Most surveys suggest that the number one complaint from teens about their parents is that their parents don't listen to them. Parents of teens say their number one desire is to listen in a way that encourages their teens to talk. So if parents want their teens to talk and teens want to talk to their parents, what's the problem?

## Listening so your teen will talk

Part of the problem is the way we listen. If we are ever going to have a lasting, meaningful relationship with our children, we need to listen in such a way that they will want to talk with us! Listening must be active, not passive. What does active listening mean? It means paying attention not just to sounds, but to facial expressions, tones of voice, emotional moods, timing, and body language. It also means making appropriate responses and asking the right questions.

We all know what it's like to finish a perfectly good and well-rehearsed lecture on the importance of the topic of, say, the value of education, and, just as we are about to make our grand finale, our young audience grunts, "Huh? Did you say somethin'?"

Now just imagine what it's like to finish a story about how your ogre-of-a-geometry teacher gave you two tons of homework just because you forgot to bring it again because the new girl asked to borrow your book right before gym which was horrible as always because you had to run like forty-eleven laps and so were sweating like crazy when the football captain bumped into you in the hall, which was like, the most embarassing moment of your life—and then your loving parent interrupts with these wise words, "Well, I'm sure it isn't as bad as you think. Could you set the table please?"

Or how about coming home late from work, plopping down in the chair that was your favorite before just now when you realize the family pet has chosen to use it as a bed, turning on the TV which is messed up again because somebody has been playing with the settings, and as you reach for your newspaper so you can sink into oblivion, an adolescent voice squeaks, "Could I have some money? I gotta go out tonight."

What about coming home from the worst day of your school career, slamming the door behind you, kicking off your stupid, ugly shoes, falling onto the couch and turning on some dumb show just to zone out for a second when your pity party is disturbed by, "Will you put your shoes in your room? I'm not your maid, you know. And how many times do I have to tell you not to slam that door!"

If you were smiling or nodding your head as you were reading these examples, then you probably know what I'm talking about. Great! That's a good place to start. On the other hand, if you feel like you're a wonderful listener or, worse, if you think the stories above were examples of perfect communication, then just listen.

What are you supposed to be listening to?

— **You**
— **Your teen**
— **Your communication together**

Many times adults irritate teens (or other adults) not with what they say, but with what they don't say, or don't even notice. When you come home after a difficult day, what do you want? What do you want people to say to you? What would you rather not hear?

Now think about your teens. What do they want to hear? Listen to the messages they're sending. Are they happy? Glum? Mad? What's their body language saying? Are their shoulders slouched? Eyes red? Heads down? How does your teen's voice sound, and why might it sound that way? What feelings are causing him to whine, groan, yell, or not talk at all?

Now are you going to think of all these questions every time you talk to your teenager? No, probably not. Good listening takes training. Maybe these three words will help you remember to listen the next time you talk to your teen.

STOP— Before you say something potentially annoying, stop and think. Is this a good time to say this? What's going on with your child? How would you feel in her situation?

LOOK—What's his body language saying? What emotions are happening? Are you keeping eye contact as you're talking?

LEARN—If you don't get the listening thing right the first, second, or twenty-fifth time, don't give up. Keep trying and learn from your mistakes. Also, learn from your teen. Learn about her—how she acts, feels, or thinks.

Now, maybe you're saying, "I do listen, he just never thinks I do." Well, then your problem may not be listening exactly, but how you listen. Maybe you can cook dinner, watch TV, wash dishes and listen to a conversation at the same time without missing anything. But maybe your teen doesn't know that. And no amount of times of you telling her, "I'm listening!" is going to change that. So what can you do?

You can practice the tricks of good listeners. Now I'm not saying you should deceive your children or anyone else. But there are some listening techniques which might help you. Most people, including teens, like to feel that they have the audience's full attention when they talk. So here are some ways to show that you are giving your full attention.

- Nod your head or say "OK," "Sure," "Oh," "I see." Use any appropriate response to affirm that you are listening. Be sincere.

- Maintain eye contact. This doesn't mean you engage in a staring match. Just be sure to look the speaker in the eyes from time to time.

- Repeat or restate what is being said. Restating what is said lets the other person know you're paying attention and helps you stay focused too. For example:

Teen:   My history teacher is so stupid!
Parent: Stupid? How come?
Teen:   He told us to read this one chapter and then he gave us a pop quiz on something completely different!
Parent: A pop quiz on a different chapter? Wow, that sounds unfair!

- Write it down. Imagine this—you talk to someone about a prayer request and then, two weeks later, that person comes back to you and gently asks about the situation. Wouldn't that feel great? Wouldn't you feel like he really cared and he had really listened? You can give that same good feeling to your teen. Maybe you have a great memory, but if you don't, after talking to your teen, write down what was said. Then after a while, casually ask about the situation. You have to be careful not to sound like you're snooping. But something like, "Hey, I was just wondering, how'd that thing work out with your friend?" might work.

We alienate our kids by passive listening. We must try to understand what they are really saying. No interrupting, no quick advice, no changing the subject to another issue. We need to give our kids the same respect we would give any other person. If we don't show them how to be good listeners, how will they ever learn to do it themselves?

# Talking so your teen will listen

The second part of the parent/teen communication problem is how we talk. How can we talk in a way that our teens will hear us? First we need to remember that we are more than just the house police. Wayne Rice, a veteran youth worker who has successfully parented three teenagers says, "Rules without a relationship lead to rebellion!"

Kids are just like the rest of us. They will be more willing to listen to and respect people who listen to and respect them. There is a great example of this in one of my favorite movies, *The Mighty Ducks*. In the movie, the coach (played by Emilio Estevez) tells the boys on the hockey team to fall on the ground; in other words, to give up and take a "dive." One of the boys refuses to cheat, saying he won't play again. Coach Bombay, realizing his own wrongdoing, apologizes to this boy. How does the coach get his message across? No pat answers. No blame shifting. No quick sermon. He apologizes, affirms the boy, and admits his own failure as a coach. This begins a deeper relationship between the two.

Rules are fine, but as in *Dead Poets Society*, rules can quickly push kids away. What we want more than anything is a relationship with our teens that models openness and trust. We have to keep up close and personal with our kids. Know what your teens are doing, what's happening in their lives. You don't need to be an adolescent psychologist to realize that parents who seek to stay involved in their kids' lives have the closest relationships with their teens.

For example, my barber recently gave up tickets to an important college football game because the event conflicted with his son's high school football game. I asked him why he chose his son's game and he said,

"Because my family comes first." Kudos to him. Sometimes the greatest opportunity for communication is just to be there for your teenager.

Communicating means spending time with your kid. Teens operate on their own time frames. We cannot rush them or the process. If your kids play sports, go to their events. If they like parks, beaches, go-carts, take them for a Teen's Nite Out. Learn to read them—their moods, their expressions, their styles.

One of the ways to do this is to think of places where your teen feels comfortable. My daughter likes to eat at a certain fast-food restaurant. So if I really want to talk with her, I take her there. While she's devouring her favorite meal, I start the conversation. Her defenses are down!

Communicating also means being open with your teen. It may be hard for your teens to open up with you if you are never open with them. How open are you when you talk with your teens? Self-disclosure is vital if we are going to develop a lifelong relationship with our kids. Don't be afraid to share your feelings. And remember that it's OK to discuss subjects that seem uncomfortable and even taboo, like sexuality, drugs, or religious beliefs. A Gallup poll of over five hundred teenagers revealed what teens wanted to discuss with their parents (Habermas and Olshine 1995: 42, 43).

| | |
|---|---|
| Family Finances: 50 percent | Politics: 39 percent |
| Drinking: 37 percent | Drugs: 35 percent |
| Sex: 23 percent | Religion: 16 percent |

The Search Institute in Minneapolis, Minnesota, surveyed teens to find out who they wanted to talk with them about sex. The overwhelming choice wasn't friends or even a trusted adult. It was parents. Teens want their parents to talk with them about sex, yet thirteen out of fourteen parents do not discuss sex with their kids (Benson 1987, 200).

## Teens do want us to talk with them— even about difficult subjects.

But how can we get these discussions started? Tim Smith insightfully writes in his book, *The Relaxed Parent,* "If you want to talk with your child, realize that you are at least 50 percent responsible. Don't blame your child for not talking with you. You have the authority and the experience that will give you a strategy for talking with your child. It's not all your fault and it's not all hers. Assume 50 percent of the responsibility, and see what happens" (1996, 141).

Read on for some more practical ideas for active communication.

# Put your answer in the form of a question

Learn something useful from the game show, "Jeopardy." Instead of delivering lectures, making accusations, or ignoring your teen, ask a question. A good question. What's a good question? A good question is one that actually allows a person the freedom to create an answer he wants to give. A good question doesn't limit a person to yes, no, or some other one-word response. A good question can start a real conversation. Here are some ideas.

### Opposite questions

Opposite questions resemble reverse psychology. For example, if your teen tells you she doesn't want to go to a classmate's birthday party, say, "Sounds like you'd like to go." Or, "Are you sure you really don't want to go?" Throwing the opposite idea at her may encourage her to open up and talk.

### Open-ended questions

"How was school today?" "Did you do anything interesting?" "How are you doing?" Questions like these will usually get answers like "Fine." "No." "Okay." Sound familiar?

Open-ended questions don't limit a person's answer. "How was school today?" is . . . fine. But a better question could be "What was the best part of your classes today?"

### Insightful, probing questions

When Rachel came home from school one day, one of her first comments was, "I got an A on my math test." I followed up her simple statement with a series of questions: "Was it easy?" "Why do you think you did so well?" "How did the rest of the class do on the test?" Probe a bit: say "It seems to me that . . ." or "I sense that you . . ." or ask "What are your thoughts on that?"

An insightful question takes a situation into account and probes beyond the surface. After hearing that your child got in trouble at school, you could ask, "What did you do?" But a better, more insightful question might be, "How did you feel when your teacher yelled at you?"

That can lead to, "Why do you think it happened?" "Who was involved?" "When is your suspension over?" (Just teasing!) Such questions open the door to further discussion rather than causing your teen to shut down.

Remember, if you don't ask, they probably won't tell. We must be the initiators of dialogue most of the time. But also keep in mind that it's not good to sound overly curious. As a youth pastor and parent, I have found that parents need to be cautious about trying to know absolutely everything about their kids' lifestyles. Do you really need to know everything? Before starting an investigation, ask yourself, will it help or hurt your relationship? Some things are better left unknown.

As a teen, there were some things I never shared with my parents because I knew that doing so would hurt them. Sometimes I just didn't think it was any of their business! When parents are too nosy, kids feel invaded. Even though our intent is to develop intimacy, excessive curiosity will cause our plan to backfire. So try to inquire without being too invasive, Sherlock!

However, your kids really do want to feel that you have enough interest in them to ask questions. To illustrate, let me tell you about my friend Ray. Ray is a youth pastor who works with troubled teenagers. Some have been in and out of jail and detention centers and many are from broken homes. One day Ray invited one of these boys with him to look at cars. Ray asked "Jeremy" his opinion: "Which car do you think I should buy?"

Jeremy responded, "I don't know. Why do you want my advice?"

Ray said, "Because you seem to know a lot more about cars than I do."

Jeremy looked somewhat puzzled. "You know," Jeremy said, "I can't ever remember an adult asking me my opinion."

That day Ray bought a car that Jeremy recommended.

Let your kids talk. Every teen needs to.

## Saying the right thing

Proverbs 15:23 says that a person "finds joy in giving an apt reply—and how good is a timely word!" Some of us have a knack for saying the right thing at the right time. Others of us have stuck our feet in our mouths so many times that we've developed a taste for tube socks. I can't tell you what to say in every situation, because I don't know you or your teen. But there are some "safe" words and classic answers. In fact, these aren't new ideas. Just read the Bible and you'll find them there!

### I'm sorry

Be quick to say, "I'm sorry." I'm sorry for yelling. I'm sorry for embarassing you. I'm sorry for being out of it. I'm sorry for not listening. I'm sorry you had a bad day. Whether or not you believe you've done something wrong, there's a good chance that just a simple, genuine "I'm sorry" will be enough to open a conversation and start a healing process between you and your teen.

### You're great!

Encouraging words can make your teen's day. Proverbs 16:24 says "Pleasant words are a honeycomb, sweet to the soul and healing to the bones." These are not just empty words of flattery but true words spoken from the mouth of someone who really knows your teen and can see all the good things about her—these are the words that should come from you, the parent. Don't wait for your teens to be down in the dumps before you lift them up. Let them know every day how important they are and how much you love them.

What about classic bad answers? I'm sure you can think of a few you know from experience. You've probably realized, for instance, that teens and adults communicate in very different ways at times. Does the following conversation look familiar?

> Parent: I'd like to sit down and chat with you.
> Teen:   (Defensive) About what?
> Parent: Nothing too heavy. I just want to see how you are doing.
> Teen:   I'm fine. (Grabs something from the refrigerator and walks out of the room)

Most teens do not want long, deep conversations with adults. If they smell even a hint of a lecture or an inquisition, they will head for the door. For most youth, several minutes is fine! Keep things down-to-earth for teenagers and learn to recognize their different learning styles. Teenagers are people in process, moving out of the child zone and into the adult world. They are influenced by media, peers, music, and parents.

Adult conversation is radically different from teen talk. Adults value in-depth dialogue and want to connect. Kids don't always value the kind of talk that adults do. So relax. If the conversation goes a solid ten minutes with a clear sense of continuity from your teen, a miracle has just occurred!

Most of us never really learned to listen and engage in dialogue until we hit our twenties. So what makes us think that a junior higher can discuss any subject with us in depth? Listen to what family counselor Norm Wright says.

Communicating with children is different from communicating with adults. Adults enjoy free and open communication, but parent-child communication is limited to the understanding of the child. Adults give, receive and carry out instructions easily. A parent must often repeatedly remind and correct a child before instructions are finally carried out (1991, 87).

One of the first lessons of communication is to know your audience. Realize that your teen is at a different stage than you are. Even his silence may mean something different from yours. Some researchers believe that it takes most teens thirty seconds to hear a question, then another thirty seconds to respond. So don't be afraid of silence. Allow for some "think" time. Don't panic. The kids are processing! (Teens especially hate it when parents ask a question and then go on to answer it themselves because the silence is awkward.)

Also, try not to talk to your teens in a demeaning way. Talking down to them will emotionally turn them off. Use reflective speaking to show that you value what they are saying and want to listen. Reflective speaking inspires the other person in the conversation to feel that she is appreciated and respected.

> Teen:   I don't know what to do about going out for cheerleading.
> Parent: You sound confused about the decision.
>
> Teen:   I hate school. Nothing went right today.
> Parent: What happened today? Sounds like you had a rough day.
>
> Teen:   I made student council.
> Parent: Are you excited? Pretty pumped up?

Notice that none of the parents offers a sermon, advice, or a quick fix. There is a question from the parent mixed in with some concern. It is what I call a "poker" comment, meaning that the intent is to "poke" inside your child's head so he or she will open up rather than shut down.

Another way to avoid communication breakdowns is to be flexible. A football metaphor often needed when parenting teenagers is the "call an audible" philosophy. Sometimes the quarterback will change the play at the line of scrimmage because he sees a weakness in the defense. As a parent, you have to be ready to adapt to your teen's changing needs. Be willing to change your communication strategy.

Communication is hard work! But the reward is priceless.

## Active T.A.L.K.

Teens really do want us to care for them. They want us to protect and provide (maybe more providing than protecting!). Adolescents want time with us—maybe not a lot of it, but some. And they want to communicate with us. You might think of your communication strategy with this acrostic.

| | | |
|---|---|---|
| T | TIME | — Spend quality time with your teen—it communicates "I love you." |
| A | AFFIRM | — Encourage. Build up, don't tear down. |
| L | LISTEN | — Eye contact, smiles and nods let them know their ideas are valued. |
| K | KNOW | — Know their world. Study them. Find ways to get inside their hearts and minds. |

## Take a risk

In 1859, a tightrope walker named Charles Blondin stretched a cable across the gorge of the Niagara Falls. He moved cautiously, going back and forth from the American side to the Canadian side, steadying himself with a forty-foot balancing pole. He performed such extraordinary tricks as crossing the cable on a bicycle, walking it blindfolded, pushing a wheelbarrow in front of him, and even cooking an omelet on a portable stove.

But his riskiest stunt took place before a hundred thousand people when he asked them if they believed that "The Great Blondin" could carry someone on his shoulders. The crowd chanted, "We believe! We believe in you, Blondin!" To which he replied, "Do I have any volunteers?"

No one responded. Silence.

Then suddenly one man shouted, "I will!" Blondin placed this man—who turned out to be his manager—on his shoulders and walked him across Niagara Falls. Six times Blondin had to take the manager off his shoulders to keep from falling!

Blondin was a risk-taker, living on the edge. When he asked for a volunteer, only one in a hundred thousand people said yes. Do we do the same thing with our teens? Do we say, "We believe in you!" but fail to follow through? Maybe we think it's too risky even to talk to our teens, to get close to them. Perhaps we think we're too boring. Out of touch. Mediocre. Blondin was careful to follow a strategy. So must we. Take risks. Do something creative. Communicate in ways that others might not even dare attempt!

# Study Session Three

## The main point

To evaluate your communication style and learn some new ways to talk with your teen.

## Think it out

Your teen comes home and says nonchalantly, "I think I'm going to drop out of school." How could you respond? Be creative. Write down all possible reactions that you could have.

## Ask yourself

1. How much time do I spend with my child on average each day?

2. What are some things we can do together that we will both enjoy?

3. What are some creative ways I can communicate authentic love to my child?

4. How can I learn more about my teen's interests?

5. What type of learner is my child? In what ways does he learn the best or the most?(through listening, doing, seeing, reading, etc.)

6. How can I help my child express what he or she is feeling?

7. What is my listening style? What are some obstacles that keep me from being a good listener?

8. Which buttons does my child push that cause me to be too emotional and defensive? Which buttons do I push that cause a similar reaction in my child?

9. Is the verbal and nonverbal communication in our home primarily uplifting or insulting? encouraging or degrading?

10. What steps could I take to be a better communicator?

**Respond to the following statements.**

I wish my teen would feel comfortable discussing _____(subject) with me. Explain why.

I wish I could discuss _____ (subject) with my teen. Think about how you might start such a conversation with your teen.

**Now be honest. Ask yourself (or better yet, ask your closest friend) to respond to this communication skills inventory. Circle all that apply.**
In general, my strengths as a listener are
    a. I am interested in people and their stories
    b. I maintain good eye contact
    c. I am an active listener
    d. I am humorous
    e. I display good body language
    f. I empathize with people
    g. other_____

My weaknesses as a listener are
    a. I am bored easily
    b. I am distracted easily
    c. I do not make eye contact
    d. I want to talk
    e. I interrupt
    f. other_____

I'd like to improve my communication skills (as related to my kids) in the following area(s):

# Look it up

Read the following verses. How does each passage relate to communication between parents and teens? Jot down your thoughts.

Exodus 20:16

Proverbs 9:7-9

Proverbs 10:19

Proverbs 12:18, 22, 23, 25

Proverbs 15:1, 4, 28

Proverbs 18:8, 13

Proverbs 25:20

Proverbs 27:5, 6

Matthew 5:33-37

Matthew 12:35-37

1 Corinthians 13:1

Ephesians 4:25, 29

Ephesians 5:4, 19, 20

James 1:19, 20

# Do something

- Role-play with your teen or your spouse at home. Read "Love-and-Logic Parenting" (p.134), "Driving You Crazy" (p.136), or "No Taboos" (p.142). Then choose a topic, either the same or different from the ones in the stories, and act out a dialogue between parents and teens. Have your teenager play the parent and you be the teen. Practice using the listening and questioning techniques discussed in this chapter.

- Track your communication habits for a week. Make a chart with space for each day. Look out for the answers to these types of questions. Then discuss your findings with your spouse, your friends, or your teen.

  When do you and your teen usually talk?
  What types of things do you talk about?
  How does your voice usually sound? tense? down? excited?
  When do you get loud?
  When do you stay silent?
  How much of what you say involves a negative? positive?

# Lift it up

Pray the prayer of the psalmist. "May the words of my mouth and the meditation of my heart be pleasing in your sight, O Lord, my Rock and my Redeemer" (Psalm 19:14). Ask God to help you find words that will help and not hurt.

# For Group Study

## Start it up

Use the "Think it out" suggestion to get discussion going. Class members could act out their reactions. Tell them to be creative and include facial expressions, body language, voice tones, etc.

## Talk it out

Divide the class into groups of three or four to discuss questions 3, 4, 6, 7, and 10 from the "Ask yourself" section. If the members of your class know each other fairly well, they could evaluate the communication styles of each other using the communication skills inventory from the self study.

Divide the verses listed on pages 64 and 65 among the groups. Give each group two or three passages to read. Allow some time for discussion about how these verses relate to communication between parents and teens. What is God telling us about how we should act toward each other through our speech? What kinds of things can we do to be more successful with our speech according to God's principles? Come together to share your findings.

## Do something

- Have another panel discussion, only this time, the parents will be the panel of "experts" and the teens will be the audience. Allow the teens to ask the parents anything they want—just make sure your parent panel is ready!

- Role-play as suggested. Let half the class be teenagers and the other half be parents.

## Lift it up

Close with prayer. Use Psalm 19:14 or some of the other verses from this study to guide your prayers.

CHAPTER FOUR

▼▼▼▼▼▼▼

# Real Conversation Is Life-Changing

We've seen that parents are the most influential factor in teens' lives and that teens do look to their parents for wisdom, advice, and models to follow. Our children's lives are shaped by the things we say and do. So, who are we following? As parents, who are we watching? What kinds of life-changing messages are our children reading through our eyes?

The best and wisest words on family relationships, raising children, and communicating can be found in one person—the ultimate parent—God. Watch your Father as he moves in your life and you will see an expert parent at work. He guides with a gentle yet strong hand. He gives us the freedom to make our own decisions, whether good or bad. Then he picks us up when we fall, without even saying "I told you so." He judges fairly, disciplines firmly, and loves unconditionally. He is the Counselor, Judge, Comforter, King, and still, he is our Father.

A hard act to follow, you say? True, but also hard to ignore. That's the whole point. Parenting is a big job. Huge. Enormous. Aren't you glad you don't have to do it alone? Isn't it a good feeling to know that God has words just for you and wants to help you? Listen to what he says:

- "For the sake of his great name the Lord will not reject his people, because the Lord was pleased to make you his own." (1 Samuel 12:22)

- "As a father has compassion on his children, so the Lord has compassion on those who fear him; for he knows how we are formed, he remembers that we are dust."(Psalm 103:13, 14)

- "My son, do not despise the Lord's discipline and do not resent his rebuke, because the Lord disciplines those he loves, as a father the son he delights in." (Proverbs 3:11, 12)

- "As a mother comforts her child, so will I comfort you; and you will be comforted over Jerusalem." (Isaiah 66:13)

- "Which of you fathers, if your son asks for a fish, will give him a snake instead? Or if he asks for an egg, will give him a scorpion? If you then, though you are evil, know how to give good gifts to your children, how much more will your Father in heaven give the Holy Spirit to those who ask him!" (Luke 11:11-13)

- "How great is the love the Father has lavished on us, that we should be called children of God!" (1 John 3:1)

God wants to be a part of his children's lives, just as much as we want to be a part of our children's lives. And since we know our children are looking to us as examples, what is it that we should be telling them, and how? God has words for us about this as well. Deuteronomy 4:9 says, "Only be careful, and watch yourselves closely so that you do not forget the things your eyes have seen or let them slip from your heart as long as you live. Teach them to your children and to their children after them." And later in Deuteronomy 6:7 we read, "Impress them on your children. Talk about them when you sit at home and when you walk along the road, when you lie down and when you get up."

The subject of God and faith may be one of the most neglected topics in our homes today. We're too busy, or too scared, or too insecure, or too worried, so we avoid topics that might be uncomfortable or complicated. But whether we actually say anything, our children are listening to the messages we send—through our actions.

The knowledge and beliefs we have about God influence every part of our lives, whether we realize it or not. Our values shape the decisions that we make about work, entertainment, health, relationships, marriage, and yes, parenting. So in a way, faith is life-changing every day. It is constantly shaping the steps that we take.

But communicating faith doesn't have to be complex or awkward. Most people don't want to be forced to believe anything, and they don't want pat answers. Our teens are the same way. So when you're trying to figure out how to communicate faith to your children, realize that God has already provided us with the best example. God came down to earth in the form of the Son, Jesus, and became one of us so we could know him better. The ways in which Jesus spoke to the people then can help us share our faith now.

The trial and crucifixion of Jesus Christ was a terrible, agonizing event. Yet probably at no other time did Jesus have such a great opportunity to spread his message to such a large number of influential people. Take a look at how he communicated the news of God's kingdom in simple, meaningful ways.

## But Jesus remained silent

There he was, on trial. His last chance to get himself out of trouble, and what did he do? Nothing. He just stood there as they brought in false witnesses who told all sorts of lies about him. But even when asked about these stories, he kept his mouth shut. Why? Why didn't he say something?

Jesus' actions that day spoke far louder than any words he could have said. If he had argued, if he had protested, if he had destroyed them all with a word as he could have done, we would not have seen the sacrifice, the submission, the love that God wants us to know.

In not speaking then, Jesus also taught us something about how to answer hostile or false words. The answer is don't. Don't give power to falsehood by arguing with it. As a parent and a child of God, your job is to let your actions reflect God's love. When given a choice (and there's always a choice), don't play with darkness when you can turn on a light. So when your children, other parents, or any other person makes false accusations or attacks you with words, don't lash back. Instead, hold your tongue, listen for the truth, and talk about it. And that brings us to the next point.

## Yes, it is as you say

Here was the big moment. You can just imagine the tension in the room as Pilate asked Jesus, "Are you the king of the Jews?" The chief priests and elders probably wore looks of disdain and sneers of bitter pleasure as the carpenter's son answered without hesitation, "Yes, it is as you say" (Matthew 27:11).

He confirmed the truth. Though he would make no reply to false accusations, this was one name he was glad to accept—King of the Jews. It was the truth. Of course he would say yes!

A second way you can communicate the good news to your children is by affirming what is true when you hear it. When you are faced with a situation that may be somewhat controversial, find the truth in it and speak to that. Point out the truth about God and his standards whenever and wherever you see it—in music, television, books, etc. Help your child to recognize the truth and have the courage to acknowledge it.

## Father, forgive them

One of the hardest things we have to learn to do whether we are parents or not is to forgive. As parents we have to learn to forgive harmful words spoken by our children, other family members, or outsiders. We have to forgive broken promises, betrayals, and disobedience. We have to look around us with all the limited knowledge we have and say, "I forgive." Wow. It's hard, isn't it?

But Jesus did it. He forgave the pain, the hurt, the sin. And listen closely to his words, "Father, forgive them, for they do not know what they are doing" (Luke 23:34). He forgave the ignorance.

That's what we have to do many times as parents. We have to look at the children we love and simply realize that they just don't know what they're doing. That doesn't mean that we ignore all their wrongdoing and shrug off their disobedience. But it does mean that we let go of anger and bitterness so that we can teach our children in a way that they can hear us.

## Into your hands I commit my spirit

Jesus never stopped placing his life in his Father's hands. With every breath, even his last on the cross, he committed his life to God.

What things are you committed to? work? sports? money? cleaning the house? ambition? image? your children? Your children notice what's valuable to you. What are you telling them?

The only way to keep our lives anywhere near the right track is to put God at the center. If you want your children to know him, make sure he's in the middle of everything you do. This may mean making certain sacrifices. Like getting up earlier or staying up later to have devotions. Or giving up a game to go to church. Or passing by an opportunity for more money to spend time at home. But these sacrifices are small if you realize that with each one, your child is seeing that what God wants is better than what the world offers.

# It is finished

Three small words. One great message.

If these words had been said by the chief priests, we would have been angry at their arrogance. If they had been said by the mourners, we would have been filled with sadness. If they had been said by Satan, we would have cringed with despair. But they were spoken by Jesus, and so we have hope.

With these three small words, Jesus announced the end of our struggle. No longer will anyone have to try to do enough good deeds to get God's attention. No longer will anyone have to attempt to cleanse himself from the sins he has committed. No longer do we have to fear death.

Notice what a difference the absence of one letter would have made. Had he said, "I am finished," there would be no words to read on this page and you wouldn't be there to read them. But "It is finished!" Can you hear the hope? Have you shown it to your kids?

The best gift anyone can give to their children is this hope in Christ. Let your children see that hope can make a difference. Let them see it by watching you not worry about small things. Let them hear it in the words you use and the enthusiasm you show. Let them know it by discovering it for themselves.

Communicating faith is not meant to be a onetime conversation delivered under pressure and guilt. It's meant to be a lifelong process. In fact, that's the whole idea of real conversations. Real conversations are real because they happen naturally, developing out of a genuine relationship that provides an environment to nurture communication. Staged conversations or "talks" that you feel you must have with your children will most likely be stiff and strange. And believe me, your teenagers will feel it.

So relax. Don't force communication on your kids. Just listen, be open, flexible, and forgiving. Commit your relationships to God's care and live your life every day with the knowledge of the hope that we have in God's love for us. Life-changing messages may be heard through the words we say, but they will be felt through the way we live.

# Study Session Four

## The main point

To evaluate the messages you are sending your teen and identify possible ways for improvement in communicating your faith.

## Think it out

Read "Legacies" on page 164. What do you want your legacy to be? Think about people who have impacted your life greatly (especially when you were young). Who were they? What did they do that had such a strong effect on you? How did they communicate their values to you?

## Ask yourself

1. Try to look objectively at your actions and words for one day. What do you think your life that day was saying about you? Your values? Your view of God?

2. How often do you discuss spiritual things such as God, the Bible, and church with your teens? How do you feel about these discussions?

3. How can you affirm truth in your daily life? What kinds of things could you point out to your children to help them see God working in their lives every day?

4. What are some ways you can show your teens that there is hope?

5. Are you and your teens able to discuss difficult subjects like sex, drugs, and drinking? Why or why not?

6. Have you and your teens talked about the future—college, marriage, parenting? What's the best way to approach these subjects? What ways should be avoided?

7. How do you and your teens communicate about issues like materialism, prejudice, financial stewardship, and integrity? Reflecting on all that you've read about conversation, what are some other ways you could communicate about these matters?

8. Do your children know what you believe about God? Have you ever asked them what they believe? What do you think they believe in?

9. How much is God a part of the relationship between you and your teens? What could you do to involve him more? Do you trust him to take care of your child?

10. How could you and your church do more to provide positive role models for teens and involve teens in ministry?

# Look it up

Since we're talking about sharing faith, it's a good idea to know what faith is. A great definition of faith is found in Hebrews 11:1: "Now faith is being sure of what we hope for and certain of what we do not see."

1. What is your hope for your children? for your family? for yourself?

2. What hope(s) can you have in God?

**Read Hebrews 11:8-12, 17-19. Answer the following questions.**

3. Look for the "even though" statements in these verses. What circumstances might have kept Abraham from doing what God asked?

4. Despite these circumstances, Abraham did what God asked. Why?

5. What makes it hard for you to be sure of what you hope for? When is it easier?

**Read Hebrews 11:13-16. Answer the following questions.**

6. Do you feel like an alien or a stranger on earth? Why or why not?

7. One of the ways we lose effectiveness in living and sharing our faith is by getting too settled in this place that is not our home. We get so caught up in desiring the things of this earth that we forget the greater hopes and dreams our Father has for us. Look at the things that take up your time. Make a list of what is most important to you. How does your list compare with the hope of heaven? If God were to make a list of his most important concerns regarding you, what do you think his list would look like?

8. People could see Abraham's faith because of the way he lived his life—even though he might have appeared crazy or strange to the people watching him! In what areas of your life do you need to be "stranger"—walking by faith, not by sight? What things of this earth do you need to let go?

## Do something

There are several ways you could share your faith with your teen. For example:

Go to church together. After the service, talk about what the message was and how you felt about it.

Study a part of the Bible with your teen. Be open to asking questions and listening to the questions of your teen.

As you watch TV with your child, ask questions about the values of the characters in the shows. Discuss what messages are being communicated and whether you agree or disagree with them. You could also do this with movies, radio, or newspaper or magazine articles. See "Music and Media" on page 116 for more ideas.

## Lift it up

Tell God about your struggles with faith and ask him to help you be strong. Lift up your teens and pray that they will continue to grow in faith.

# For Group Study

## Start it up

Read "Legacies" on page 164. Divide into groups of three or four. Share stories about people who have impacted your lives greatly (especially as children). Who were they? What did they do that had such a strong effect?

## Talk it out

Remain in groups and discuss questions 3, 4, 7 and 9. After some time, have groups share the main points of their discussions.

Read the verses from Hebrews and use the questions provided from the "Look it up" section for discussion.

## Do something

- Have a faith walk. Put blindfolds on some and choose others as leaders. Set up an obstacle course. Have the leaders use voice directions to guide the others through the course. Talk about the feelings each group had. What was difficult? What made it easy?

- Divide the class into groups of five or six. Each group will be an advertising team. Have them design a persuasive television commercial that promotes faith in God. The ads can be no longer than two minutes. Be creative! You may want to provide markers and poster board or paper.

  After the ads have been shown, discuss which one was most persuasive. Then discuss how Christianity is appealing or not to the general public. How can we accurately show our teens what faith is about?

## Lift it up

Close the session with prayer. Ask for the courage and commitment needed to help communicate faith to your children.

# Part Two

# Real Parents

## Be Real

*Ask any kid what he or she appreciates about an admired adult and you'll hear something like, "He really cares," or "She's just so real." Adolescents are experts at detecting fabricated, insincere behavior. To every overture you make, they apply their own polygraph tests to detect your authenticity.*

*Unfortunately, I have seen too many mature adults who think being real requires them to act in ways that are not parental. Nothing could be further from the truth. Being real is about earning trust. It's about being who you are all the time, not stepping into a "real" role. In short, being real means not being its opposite—acting in a way that's false to you.*

Les Parrott

# You're Number One

In sports, at any level, most fans ultimately ask: "Who's number one?" "What do the polls say?" "Who will win it all?"

Here's great news for parents: When it comes to the most important issues of life, you're the most important people to teens. Your influence in their lives is the most significant. There's not even a close "second best" in their opinion.

A few years ago, the Search Institute polled over eight thousand young teens and more than ten thousand parents to determine who kids turn to for their really important values. Where do the most critical influences come from?

For instance, when young teens were asked who they would seek for serious advice concerning help for their friends who were using drugs and alcohol, 40 percent claimed they would ask Mom or Dad; only 16 percent said they would go to other friends.

Also, surprising to some, when these same early adolescents were polled about issues on sexual education, parents came out way ahead. If teens had questions about sex, 50 percent of them would go to parents; only 20 percent would rely on peers.

Finally—and most dramatically—when deciding what to do with their lives, 63 percent of youth indicated they would call on their parents first. Only 8 percent would choose friends (Benson 1987, 200).

Pretty reassuring, huh?

You're more important than you may realize. When the chips are down, your kids look to you. They know they can count on you. Your advice. Your conversations.

You're number one in the nation. Season after season. Perennial champs!

# Parent's Psalm 23

*Matt Wilmington*

You are my parent,
I shall not want any other caregiver.
You meet all my needs,
you provide a quiet, peaceful home,
you encourage my soul.

You guide me, by your own life, in paths of
righteousness.
Even though I walk through the valley of
puberty, temptation, rejection, and failure,
I will fear no evil,
for you always have time for me.
Your decisions, character, and discipline—
they each comfort me.

You provide a refreshing alternative for me
in the presence of the world, the devil, and
my own culture;
you lavish me with blessings;
my life overflows.

Surely goodness will lead me
and follow me all the days of my life.
And I will always be glad that
I was a member of your household.

# Make Every Shot Count

Many men and women have impacted our world for good.

- John Bunyan, who guided the progress of millions of pilgrims
- Leonardo da Vinci, who inaugurated the Renaissance
- Henry Ford, whose invention drives you and your teenagers crazy!
- Benjamin Franklin, whose invention, eyeglasses, enables many people to read
- Martin Luther, the radical thinker who began the Protestant Reformation
- Alexander Pope, the most accomplished verse satirist in the English language
- William Shakespeare, the best playwright of all time
- Eli Whitney, who gave us the cotton gin
- Mother Teresa, who gave dignity to the poor and dying in the streets of Calcutta, India

The good news is that you don't need to be Beethoven, Lincoln, Churchill, or Amy Grant to make a difference in society. Simply be yourself! God uses extraordinary people and ordinary people—one at a time. You *can* make a difference.

As a parent, you have the power to change the world perhaps more than any other group—more than teachers, ministers, politicians, or athletes. You are shaping a human being. Wow!

So make every moment count.

When I was young, I played a lot of basketball in our backyard. I spent many hours working on my free throws. My dad would tell me, "Take your time. Make every shot count."

Good advice. Parents, you have a limited number of opportunities to impact your kids for good. Make them count! The time spent raising a kid goes so fast that if you are not careful, it will pass you by.

Repeat this often to yourself: "I am making a huge contribution to this world. I will—by God's grace—invest my energies in developing the best child possible for the planet. May God use my child to bring about his purposes on earth."

Mom and Dad, you are the number one influence in your teen's physical, emotional, and spiritual growth. You are not just important—you are *the most important* people affecting the welfare of your children. When the pressure is on, your kids look to you. So next time you stand below the basket, make your shot count.

# From a Mentor

*Brian Richardson*

Say
Are you looking at me?
Are you trying to understand
a friend who's nearby,
with helping hands?
A person with whom you can
confide your plans?
Please understand that sometimes I fall.
The cliff of deceit is not
far from us all.
It shades and disguises
the pitfalls of sin,
it smothers the love that
New Life begins.
So I pose, again,
this question with fright:
Will you carefully observe me
throughout the long nights?
If so, watch me and pray for me
and I'll do the same.
Don't cast your blame,
just take it easy—you know—
day by day
And let's watch what we
say.

# Hands-on Parenting

In the winter 1997 issue of *Fantastic Flyer* magazine, John Shirey, city manager of Cincinnati, Ohio, describes his priorities as a husband and a father.

> When our first child was born, my wife and I decided that she would not go back to work outside the home but would stay with our daughter.
>
> Three children and fifteen years later, this still works for us. If it is possible for one parent to be at home—whether it be the mother or the father—it makes a tremendous difference, especially in the first five years of a child's life.
>
> When we decided to try and live on one income, we were not well-off, but my wife, Marilyn, and I were committed to being hands-on parents. We never assumed that, just because we were biologically able to be parents, we knew how to parent. We studied. My wife bought books on parenting. . . . For parents, communication with their children usually means listening. Not a day goes by that we don't ask what's going on in our children's lives. They feel they can talk to us about their school, friends, and homework. Even our fifteen year old opens up, which, as parents of teenagers know, is a miracle (Shirey 1997, 34)!

Hands-on parenting is involved parenting. I am amazed at how many times after my parenting seminars, parents complain about how little time they have with their children. As they explain, it's obvious that the parents are too busy and not in control. Dad works too much. Mom's overextended. The kids participate in every activity possible.

We are more than protectors, providers, chauffeurs, laundry robots, chefs, etc. Hands-on parenting is making the decision to be with your kids, not just do for your kids.

A friend of mine, "Mark," was invited to teach by a prestigious university in California. It would mean a greater salary and a higher profile. Mark and his wife struggled with the decision. They prayed, knowing they would have to uproot their children, with their teenager ready to graduate in a few years. They chose not to go. Why?

A big raise and national recognition did not do it for Mark and his wife. They chose to live in a slow-paced, small, midwestern town that keeps their family from a rat-race existence. "I didn't want to spend three hours a day in a car on the expressway in L.A." said Mark. "I knew if we moved to California, there would be stresses for me and my family that we might not be ready for. Plus, I want to be at home every night and the move to southern California would have been a workaholic position. I'd feel like I was an absentee father."

Call it time at home. Call it priorities. Call it focus on his family. Call it hands-on parenting. Are there decisions you need to make to be a hands-on parent?

## It Takes Time

*Brian Richardson*

Can someone over fifty years old relate to teens today? Face it, we live in different worlds. Actually, solar systems. But recently a thirteen-year-old girl said to me, "I love you. You are just like a grandfather to me." Why? Her family spent a weekend with my family. I gave her and her brother my undivided attention. When they asked, "Will you take us fishing?" I grabbed the gear and said, "Let's go." The three of us spent the day together. Teens—like all of us—need someone willing to relate one-on-one. Someone who believes we are important enough to invest the time. At that point, age doesn't matter. We simply need someone who cares.

# Dealing With Divorce

Divorce. My parents told me the news the night I returned from eight weeks of summer camp. My dad turned off the TV. I said, "Hey, what'd you do that for?" His painful words came slowly, "David, we have something to tell you. Your mother and I are getting a divorce." I ran out of the room crying. I was twelve years old, had just hit puberty, and now my parents were splitting up. My world caved in.

I call that time the triple punch. The first punch was puberty. My voice was changing, and my hormones were wild. The second punch was being told that the unthinkable—divorce—had entered my young world. The final blow came later that night. My mom told me that she and I were going to move to a state five hundred miles away. After living in the same house all my life, I was being uprooted from all that I had ever known. The familiar faces and places evaporated in a matter of days.

Maybe divorce has knocked you down, and you've been feeling the blows ever since. To make matters worse, you probably feel guilty, angry, and all alone. The fear of raising a teenager is overwhelming. If you are a single parent or remarried, here are four ways to help you and your teen get through the horrific experience of divorce.

*Take care of yourself.* Some divorced parents are so burned out from helping their kid(s) adjust to the trauma of divorce that they have little energy left to relax and improve their own well-being. Make an effort to get well. Spend time alone, if necessary. Join a twelve-step group or a Bible study. Exercise. Get some extra sleep.

*Resist "triangle games" between your children and your ex.* A triangle often occurs when two people cannot resolve a conflict. So they bring in a third person to ease the tension. The sad fact is that when divorce happens, the teenage child is often that third person. Teens regularly hear from one or both parents how awful the other parent is. Most teens do not have the emotional maturity to be the third side of such a triangle. They feel that they must align with one parent. Then, the other parent gets more irritated and blames the kid. It ends up being a lose-lose scenario. Resist triangles. If you have a conflict with your former spouse, discuss it directly with him or her, not your child.

*Let your teens know that the divorce was not their fault.* Children of divorce carry an enormous amount of guilt over their parents' separation. This is even true for teens who intellectually know they had nothing to do with the breakup. Children need to hear straight from you—the parent—that they were not the problem.

*Keep the lines of communication open with your teen.* If you have remarried, recognize that this is a major life transition and it's stressful for you, your new spouse, and your children—especially for your teenage children. A blended family means different rules, boundaries, and habits. The new love in your life may arouse some jealousies in your children. Reassure your kids of your love. Don't expect them to transfer their allegiance to their new stepfather or stepmother as quickly as you did. In fact, your kids may not be able to call your new spouse "Mom" or "Dad" right away—or ever. It takes time. Emotions swing up and down. There will be highs of resentment and lows of apathy. Listen to your kids. Listen to their hurts, their concerns, and their questions. If you sense anger, ask them what is really bothering them.

## Remember the Snowflakes

*Mark H. Senter III*

It is funny how good memories block out the memory of pain. This afternoon, as Ruth and I walked through snow flurries at Colorado's Lost Valley Ranch, my mind drifted back to a similar experience: snow showers at a Pioneer Camp near the Canadian Rockies. There, we rode on horseback through the wet snowflakes, catching glimpses of the Canadian Rockies in the distance. Memories of the velvet quiet of snow-covered pines and the warmth of the horse's strong body rushed into my mind.

Then came another recollection. During that same beautiful setting in Canada, I had been as sick as a dog. I had flown from Chicago to Calgary and traveled two hours by car to a camp where I spoke to a group of youth workers. The further I traveled and the longer I spoke, the sicker I became. After the sessions, the groups had scheduled a horseback ride. My choice was simple. Lie in a cabin and be sick or experience the beauty of the trail ride and be sick. I chose the latter.

I guess building good memories—and recalling them—is a choice, whether on a horse in Alberta or in the daily stress of family routines. It's not so much what happens to you that counts, but how you respond.

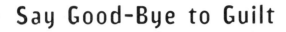

# Say Good-Bye to Guilt

A woman stands before some self-righteous men. They believe she is a sinner. They are critical of her lifestyle and proud of their holiness. Listen to the Pharisees' words to Jesus: "Teacher, this woman was caught in the act of adultery" (John 8:4). From private seduction to public embarrassment. People stare at her. Some run from her. Most gossip. Her reputation is disgraced. She is shunned and ridiculed. These spiritual leaders continue: "In the Law Moses commanded us to stone such women. Now what do you say?" (8:5).

It's Jesus' turn. But what does he do? He starts writing on the ground. Yes, he writes on the ground with his finger. Finally he looks up and says, "If any one of you is without sin, let him be the first to throw a stone at her" (8:7).

The elders are the first to drop their rocks and go. Eventually, they all leave. All but two: Jesus and the adulteress. He speaks, "Neither do I condemn you. Go now and leave your life of sin" (8:11).

How does God respond when you blow it? We parents make mistakes every day. Nobody said it would be easy. How do we get rid of the guilt of poor decisions and unresolved conflict?

God responds to us as he did to the woman in John 8: "Neither do I condemn you." Put these words on your bedside table or on your refrigerator. How do you remove the G word? You don't have to. Jesus did. And he did it for you and me. His cross carries the message: No more guilt.

Say no to guilt. Ask and receive forgiveness, Mom, for the time you reacted out of anger instead of love. Be forgiven, Dad, for the time you promised you'd be at your son's basketball game but got stuck in a meeting. Kiss the G word good-bye.

# Good Intentions?

*Les Parrott*

In his play, *Murder in the Cathedral*, T.S. Eliot wrote, "The greatest sin is to do all the right things for all the wrong reasons." He may be right, but it's just as sinful to do all the wrong things for all the right reasons. A young person's budding faith can easily be damaged by a parent's good intentions. Here's one example: Don't use guilt to motivate your son or daughter. You may mean well, but few people grow from that strategy. Examine your words and actions thoroughly. Are you pushing some guilt buttons?

# Be Vulnerable

I should have stayed in bed on the first Friday in January.

Instead, I woke up at 6 A.M., drove forty miles, spent three hours doing jury duty, and got in a car accident. Then, I was hungry. So I headed for the nearest fast-food restaurant.

"Hamburger, without onions," I ordered.

After finding a quiet corner of the room, I sat down with a deep sigh. I opened the wrapper and exclaimed, "Well, that just about does it!" loud enough for two startled patrons twenty feet away to turn their heads. What they didn't see was that I had a hamburger *with* onions.

Just then I noticed one of my former students enter with a handful of teens. "Should I say hi or just ignore him?" I asked myself. I wasn't in the mood for friendly conversation. "Oh, it wouldn't hurt," the generous part of me said. "I'm not sure I have the energy or motivation," the stressed-out part countered. Within seconds, the friendly side won.

"Hey, Brian!" I shouted. "What are you doing here?"

"I'm taking a few kids from our church out to lunch, then over to their basketball practice. See those two girls?" he asked, motioning toward where they were ordering. "They're two of the greatest eighth-grade student leaders I've ever seen. Super potential!"

"Cool," I responded, in a mostly uninterested spirit.

When Brian asked how my day was going, I said, "Pray for me." Then I gave him a brief report of my morning woes.

"I will pray for you," this youth pastor promised. Then he went back to his teens, and I went back to my onion-topped burger.

In a matter of seconds, I heard two young voices behind me.

"Hi, I'm Stacey."

"And I'm Kelly." In sync, they extended their hands in greeting.

"Pastor Brian told us you're an awesome teacher of his and that you're having a bad day."

Somewhat embarrassed, I responded, "Yeah, and I also got these onions after I told them to hold them."

"Don't you just hate it when that happens?" Kelly jumped in.

"Well, we're just here to cheer you up," both said in unison. "Hope you have a better afternoon." They waved and returned to their group.

"That's what Christian encouragement is about," I said to myself. "I really needed that!"

Then it hit me. I would not have even been the recipient of that fantastic, unexpected greeting if I had not spoken up, if I had not been vulnerable enough to share my needs.

Teens can encourage you. They can make your day. But it must start with you: your expectations, your vulnerability, your open communication.

Be honest with your kids. Ask them to pray for you. Model how to be vulnerable. Then, listen as your "Stacey" and "Kelly" encourage you.

## Healthy Balance

*Les Parrott*

When the scales of a relationship are unbalanced—when one person is always receiving and the other is always giving—both people eventually feel cheated. In healthy relationships, people meet each other's needs. There is give and take that keeps both people in balance. Allow your teen to care for you as much as you care for him or her. Don't fall into the trap of thinking that you aren't a good parent unless you do all the giving. After all, how else will youth learn to give? Is there anything in your present relationship that indicates that the scales are tipped unnecessarily? What needs to be done to balance them?

# ▶ Real Teens ◀

## *In Their Sneakers*

*To build good relationships, you must learn to see the world from other people's perspectives. The fancy word for this is empathy, and it can unlock a million mysteries. Once you put yourself in your kids' sneakers you begin to understand why they react, feel, and think the way they do. Of course, empathy does not come naturally or quickly. Like anything that's noble, it requires time and effort. It starts with a simple decision to see life as your youth sees it. Good, open-ended questions signal your willingness to cultivate a healthy relationship with your teen. But, is it worth such an investment? you might ask. All I can say is that the relational dividends of empathy are well worth it. The payoffs are overwhelming.*

Les Parrott

# Know Your Teen

Recognize. Distinguish. Specify. This is what it means to know something. When the Bible speaks of Adam knowing Eve, the reference is to one that knows "intimately and experientially." God wants us to know our teens.

Any parent of two or more kids quickly realizes that no two children—even twins—are the same. Personalities, gifts and talents, height, temperament, IQ, opportunities, communication skills, desires, voices, fingerprints, hair and eye color, attitudes—each teen is fearfully and wonderfully made. And unique.

Consequently, the way we attempt to inform, motivate, encourage, and discipline our kids must vary from child to child. Demonstrating love falls into the same category. That's where knowing comes in. Some teens value verbal statements of love. Others favor nonverbal expressions. Some like to be kissed and hugged, but others (often guys) prefer shoulder punches, high fives, or a neck rub.

What complicates our job description as parents is that what appears to be cool and acceptable communication today is uncool and unacceptable tomorrow! So just when you think you know your teens inside and out, you recognize that there is a lot more to know about them.

Keep in touch with them—literally. Be sensitive to what turns their cranks and what repulses them. "A gentle answer turns away wrath, but a harsh word stirs up anger" (Proverbs 15:1).

Recognize. Distinguish. Specify. Know your teen.

# Custom Teen Care

*Brian Richardson*

The need to observe teens—to really study them—is undeniable. Of course, one of the reasons is because they're unique. Kinda like looking at a car. You care for cars differently, depending on what they've been through. Some autos have seen a lot of mud, and you must spend the bulk of your time cleaning, not detailing. Others require only a gentle cleaning—no need to dull the finish. Still other cars need wax and polish to prepare them for the rough weather ahead. The same is true of teens. Before grabbing the bucket and sponge, stand back and first determine each individual's particular need.

# Mood Swings

At the Olshine household, we have had a long-standing tradition. During dinner together (which is another tradition that we keep), someone says, "Best part of the day." Hands go up. The last person to raise her hand must share the best part of her day. After she is finished sharing, within several minutes she will say, "Best part of the day" and the game is repeated until all have shared.

It's a game we made up to keep communication ongoing and alive. Now that we have a teenager in our midst, the game has taken on new meaning. It can be like a roller coaster emotionally. Some days the sharing is upbeat, and other times it is a bit unsettled. Mood swings.

All teens experience moodiness. Dr. Bruce Narramore writes, "It is the rare person who moves from the dependency of childhood to the independence of adulthood without passing through stretches of troubled water on the way" (1980, 36).

Maybe you have never taken an Adolescent 101 class or gone to a parenting graduate school. Well, here is one of the first lessons to understand: Mood swings are normal in adolescence. Don't freak out or panic. Enjoy the good moods and watch the signs for the bad ones. Your teen will show his mood more than tell you about it. You may read a bad mood by his droopy shoulders or deadpan face.

If you notice a bad mood, carefully inquire. Some possible questions might be:

- Are you upset with me?
- Is there something you need that I can help you with?
- What has happened to irritate you?

Unless there is chronic depression, mood swings rarely necessitate seeing a counselor or therapist. Usually, the moods are correlated to the new biological changes of pubescence. Relax and enjoy the pendulum.

# Fear Today, Gone Tomorrow

*Mark H. Senter III*

Our grade school athlete was terrified of thunderstorms. Storm warnings would send his scare-o-meter into the red zone. Tornado watches were worse. At the first clap of late-night thunder, he could hardly refrain from diving into bed between my wife and me, in search of a safe place.

All this changed one night near Jackson Hole, Wyoming. We were camping with some friends when, in the middle of the night, a thunderstorm struck that sounded like a freight train passing within inches of our tent. Wind and rain drove at the flimsy canvas. I waited for our storm-hater to make his move. But he never did. Curled up in his sleeping bag, he slept right through the storm.

In the morning, as we hung up our dampened sleeping bags, I asked what he thought of the storm. He replied, "That was something, wasn't it?" In fact, he never again had any fear of thunderstorms. He grew up that night in the tent. Funny how we parents often think that some problem our teen has been struggling with might last forever and a day. Then—overnight—it's resolved.

# Accounting for Taste

All of us make decisions based on our own personal tastes. On a recent trip to our local mall, I relearned this valuable lesson.

Upon entering the mall, everyone had a different plan about how to spend the morning. So, we scheduled a rendezvous at noon in the food court.

There, again, everybody had a different preference for lunch. Susie, our twelve year old, selected her favorite, a slice of cheese pizza. Melissa, our sixteen year old, chose a club sandwich from the submarine shop. Twenty-year-old Elizabeth opted for the Philly cheesesteak. Their mom took the classic gyro from the Greek cuisine expert. And I settled for the all-American hamburger.

Thankfully, we at least decided to eat together—but we spent the first five minutes debating who made the best choice!

That experience got me thinking about how personal preference influences much of what we do—and how parents need to sensitively modify their language and treatment of each child, based on those preferences.

Just think about a few of the multitude of preferences we have:

- Foods
- Colors
- Clothing styles
- Learning and teaching styles
- Friends
- Books and other reading materials
- Sports
- TV programs
- Vocation
- Leisure time

It comes down to this: when we recognize our own preferences in our conversations, we need to remember that our children have preferences too. God has created each person in a unique way. Each person is a creation of God—one of a kind.

# Nocturnal Animals

*Jana L. Sundene*

One of my favorite zoo animals is the bush baby. A bush baby is a nocturnal animal that has a Yoda-like face on the body of a flying squirrel. What a combo! The critters appear suddenly from their hiding places in hollowed logs and literally leap from one side of the cage to the other—bing, bing! Occasionally they come right up to the glass, stare at you, then leap away. Most people I know have never seen a bush baby for one simple reason—you must be willing to wait ten to thirty minutes for them to appear. Does this remind you of teens? They come alive at night, full of energy, and then disappear. We miss important opportunities to interact with them, unless we're willing to wait patiently—in their territory—for them to come into view.

# Growing Up

Forty-eight inches. Four feet.

That arbitrary distance divided childhood from adolescence for my oldest daughter, Elizabeth. Several summers ago, our family visited an amusement park—but not just any amusement park.

At typical theme parks it is standard practice to display signs that say visitors are prohibited from riding most attractions unless the visitors are a certain height. Well, the park we went to catered to young kids so those rules were reversed.

"Sorry, Elizabeth," we told our preteen more than once that day. "Here's another sign that says you have to be less than forty-eight inches tall to get on this ride."

So, there she was, caught in between. No longer a child, yet not quite a teenager, Elizabeth stood idly by and watched her two younger sisters enjoy some of the park rides by themselves.

"It's not fair!" I remember our oldest saying repeatedly that day.

"No, you're right," I feebly replied.

That was a turning point for Elizabeth. It was as though she was forced to become a teen overnight. From that point on she did less and less kid stuff and more and more youth stuff. From fewer kids' rides to more excursions with her friends. From fewer kiddy fashions to more grown-up cosmetics. From fewer comic books to more Christian romance novels. There was no turning back.

Such growth stages can sometimes be more traumatic for parents than for their children. "Where did all those years of innocence go?" a parent may wonder in a melancholy manner. "Why do they have to grow up so fast?"

Or, a parent may decide to look on the bright side: "What incredible possibilities does God intend for my child? How will he continue to shape her personality? What role should I play in this entire process?"

It seems to me that the parents who choose the latter perspective—to see life's potential through their child, rather than unsuccessfully attempt to freeze time—will stand a far better chance of helping both themselves and their teen through these years of inevitable change.

Consider the area of communication. Parents who (even silently) wish that their kid would never grow up communicate uncertainty and anxiety. Nothing new is ever acceptable compared with the "good ol' days." In the end, trying to freeze time only freezes character building—for both parent and child.

Conversely, the parent who faces the future in a positive fashion conveys confidence to his offspring. A "what-will-today-bring?" message of hope in your conversation will go a long way in your home. Not only is such an attitude more upbeat than the earlier scenario, but it also fosters other positive rewards. One of the best effects may be an invitation from your teenager to initiate future dialogue, especially in tough times.

## The Emperor Penguin Principle

*Duffy Robbins*

I first uncovered the "Emperor Penguin Principle" while leafing through a magazine. There, on the page in front of me, was a male emperor penguin with an egg balanced precariously on his feet. Not being well-versed on the specifics of penguin husbandry, I read the caption. It said that the male emperor penguin warms the egg while the female fattens herself on fish from the Antarctic waters. The article went on to explain that when the female emperor penguin lays her egg, she gingerly rolls it over to her mate, who places it on his feet for two months until it hatches!

How many times, as a parent, have I felt like an emperor penguin? I want to see my children grow and mature into all that God wants them to be. But why must this process of growing up go so slowly? Perhaps the best reason is the one implicit in what I call the "Emperor Penguin Principle": Genuine and thorough growth takes time. And one of the main demands of parenting is our willingness to trust God. And to simply wait.

# Let Kids Be Kids

In 1 Corinthians 13:11, the apostle Paul declares a remarkable personal testimony: "When I was a child, I talked like a child, I thought like a child, I reasoned like a child. When I became a man, I put childish ways behind me."

In this brief commentary, Paul provides at least two useful directives for parents. First, Paul states that children (and teens) are distinct from adults. "We all know that!" you might be tempted to shout. But he is not so much referring to fads, personalities, and preferences as he is to biological differences. He is claiming that—at their very core—kids and adults are unique. Specifically, Paul is declaring both age groups—children and adults—to be inherently valuable. Each has a place. One group is not to judge the other.

To rephrase it, Paul says, "I was a child and that was good."

Second, the apostle concludes that if adults revert to acting like children, immaturity results, since "childish ways" should have been put behind them. Note here that the author is carefully distinguishing between childlikeness (what is appropriate for kids to be) and childishness (what is inappropriate for adults to be).

The opposite of this last point is also crucial for parents of teens. Just as it's inappropriate for adults to act in childish ways, it's equally wrong for children and teens to be expected to act in fully adult ways.

As you communicate with your teens through spontaneous talks and planned strategies of parenting, be certain that you're not rushing your youth too quickly into adulthood. Help them to feel comfortable with their adolescent years. Treat them fairly for who they *are*, not for who they may become.

# Gangs and Growth

*Matt Wilmington*

The fifty students I had brought to inner-city Chicago waited nervously in the church classroom. Finally, fourteen local gang members strode into the room for a prearranged question-and-answer session. For the next two hours they articulated with great passion their need for their gang. The gang members loved and protected each other. They even helped each member at school. As illogical as some of their answers seemed regarding gang violence and drugs, one truth emerged: Teenagers need each other.

Whether you call it a gang, a clique, a team, or whatever, adolescents require the support of their peers. Groups your teens "hang with" mirror who they are, and serve as a map for where they want to go. Try to guide your teens into positive peer associations. As they establish their own identities and move from an inherited faith to a personal faith, that positive group of friends will help them move on to the next leg of their spiritual journey.

# More Than Meets the Eye

A few years ago, my wife informed me that our ninth grader at the time, Melissa, was "third chair flute" in our local high school band ("third chair" means third best among those particular instruments, sitting literally in the third chair away from the top performer of her section of the band). Our high school band is huge. They have, for example, twelve kids playing flute. So it's quite an accomplishment for a freshman to make third chair.

When we went to the school's annual Christmas program, it took me a moment to locate my daughter, for she wasn't sitting where I expected.

"One, two, three," I counted under my breath, thinking that was all I needed to count. "Four? Five?" I hesitantly added.

I turned to my wife with a puzzled look. "I thought you said that Melissa was 'third chair.'"

"I did," she replied, with that "don't-you-get-it-yet?" look.

"Well, why, then, is she seated in the fifth chair? Am I missing something here?"

"Yes, we're both missing the concert," Mary answered. "But, if you have to know just now," she continued, "there were two flute players tied for second, and then Melissa and another girl tied for third!"

"Oh, so 'third' really means 'fifth,'" I deftly concluded.

"Exactly."

That brief conversation helped me realize how important perspectives are. Specifically, I understood the significant place that perspectives have for parents when it comes to their teens.

As caregivers, we need to consistently see our youth in the very best light. We need to give them the benefit of the doubt in our discussions. We need to express to them how proud we are of them—always keeping their best interests in mind.

And, yes, that even means bending the absolute rules of math just a bit—calling "fifth place" "third place"—if it strengthens our ties with them.

## Video Values

*Jim Mohler*

A camera freezes a single moment in time. It takes a snapshot for us to enjoy later. But snapshots don't provide the before and after. It's easy to become discouraged when we choose to use only snapshots, figuratively speaking, while capturing special moments in our teen's life. Before you totally invest in that approach, consider the video alternative. Videos value process as well as product. They focus not just on landmark events or accomplishments (like a once-in-a-lifetime sixteenth birthday), but they also focus on how the teen got there (i.e., the awkward, often spontaneous times leading up to maturity). So, when someone asks how your teen is doing, ask, "Do you want to see the photo album or the video library?"

# Mall Mania

*Our fourteen year old seems bored frequently and wants to spend a lot of time at the mall. She wants to go there with her friends, and asks us to drop her off for several hours. What is your opinion?*

*Sincerely,*

*Frustrated*

Dear Frustrated,

Many teens feel "called to the mall." The problem is this: What kind of trouble (besides overspending) lurks behind the corner? As a dad with a daughter, what bothers me more than a teenage girl wanting to spend a day at the mall are some of the sleazy and surly teenage guys that hang around there. Do you know what I mean? They look like accidents waiting to happen! I really don't want my daughter in that kind of atmosphere without some parental "eyes" on the scene.

Why not suggest that just the two of you have a weekly date at the mall? This could mean shopping together, or having her bring a friend and you meeting them after an hour of separation. That could meet her mall need.

Or try solving her boredom problem in a different way. I recommend that your child develop some kind of hobby. Involve your child in sports, or some other activity to help her use her energy.

Another problem is that your fourteen year old doesn't have a driver's license, which means you are the taxi service. I suggest you say, "I'm glad you want to hang out with some of your friends. Why don't you have them over to the house this weekend for a slumber party, or for an evening to eat pizza and watch a video?"

Finally, if the real issue is that your daughter needs some breathing room away from you, then work out a plan that involves a number of options. For example, perhaps you and your husband can agree that on Wednesday evenings your daughter can spend two hours with friends. Suggest alternatives to the mall. It might be a movie one week and rollerblading the next. Let her know you trust her, yet give her some parameters so she can prove she is responsible.

# Give Them the Power

*David Veerman*

Good managers delegate, giving their staff important and appropriate responsibilities. A mistake that some make, however, is to delegate responsibility but not authority. Staff members need to know that they have the authority to make decisions without always having to check with the boss. Parents can use this lesson too. As kids get older, they also need to learn skills and to take responsibility. So, what do we parents do? We give them important jobs. We delegate. But to grow, they need more than major responsibilities—they need appropriate authority—both the power and the freedom to make their own decisions.

# Acne Attack!

Zits. Ugh! Some communication tactics work well and some don't work at all when it comes to helping our pimply-faced teens look in the mirror every morning. Have you ever said to your teen:

- If you keep eating chocolate, you'll get pimples.
- Don't worry, nobody will see it.
- If you pop that pimple it might scar, and then everyone will stare at you for the rest of your life.
- Make sure you wash your face before you go to bed.
- Everybody gets pimples; even Grandpa once had them.

Not all medical practitioners agree on what causes acne. Most doctors think a physical predisposition to acne, poor hygiene, stress, lack of sunlight, and increased hormone levels brought on by puberty all play a role.

We know that nobody likes zits. Breakouts happen at the most inconvenient times of life—like before the prom—and in the most noticeable places—like between our eyes or on our foreheads! Some teens get pimples constantly; others hardly ever. Teens are more appearance conscious than any other age group, so we need to proactively communicate with them about acne. How?

1. Encourage lots of soap and showers.
Sound elementary, Dr. Watson? A ten year old may be able to go days without a shower, but not a thirteen year old! Encourage your kids to wash their faces every morning and evening.

2. If the acne worsens, seek medical help.
If you notice the acne is getting worse, head to the drugstore for some over-the-counter medicine. Many medications will dry up the blemishes in a matter of days. If the condition does not improve, find a competent dermatologist. Some kids need medical treatment.

3. Don't nag—teens are already self-conscious about it.
A number of years ago, a parent of a teen in my youth group kept nagging her teenage girl to clean her face. Nag, nag, nag, nag, nag. The girl became so irritated that she stopped talking to her mom for three days! Finally her mother apologized for being insensitive. She recognized that their relationship was more important than harping about zits.

4. Err to the side of positive strokes, not put-downs.

You are called to be a parent, to come alongside your teen as a guide, a consultant. Too often we become our kids' police officers, prison wardens, and army sergeants, which only encourages them to rebel. Criticism can hurt, and when it comes to appearances, teens take negative comments personally! My mom offered a wise axiom as I grew up: If you have nothing nice to say, don't say anything at all.

Affirm how your kids look and dress. If you need to occasionally disagree with their clothing, hairstyle, or appearance, say something such as: "I understand your desire to _____, but it is inappropriate in this situation. I am sure you can _____ on another occasion." Keep your comments upbeat and optimistic.

## Diamond in the Rough

*Brian Richardson*

Standing in the line at the grocery store the other day, I overheard a conversation between a mother and what appeared to be her sixteen-year-old daughter. "Just think," the mom began, "in another month you'll be a teenager!" I almost fell through the floor! Teens often develop physically before they have the emotional, social, and spiritual maturity to handle the hormones that drive them. And yet these hormonal changes directly affect their entire being. What to do? Have patience. Listen. And, above all, picture your teen as a roughly-cut diamond— beautiful in some areas, jagged in others. But always very precious.

# Jobs

Should your teenager work outside the home? Some people believe that part-time work is fine for late adolescents. Others believe that thirty hours a week is acceptable. A number of parents don't want their kids to get jobs until college.

One family I know has a three-point philosophy on their kids working. If their children can uphold these three Rs, they can work outside of school and/or participate in extracurricular activities (which are really jobs outside of school and home—they don't pay but they take up a lot of time):

**Reality—do regular household chores**
**Reason—maintain a B average**
**Respect—honor and communicate respect to all family members**

I recently came across an old USA Today article that chronicled the story of Khalid El-Amin, then a 5' 11" point guard for Minneapolis North High School (he's now playing for the University of Connecticut). El-Amin led the team to two consecutive state titles. The article read as follows: "When report cards came out Monday, Charles and Arlene El-Amin informed North coach, Robin Ingram, that their son, among the most-recruited high school players in Minnesota history, will not play again until his grades improve. The two-time all-stater was averaging 20 points and seven assists for the Polar Bears (8-2) this season" (January, 1997).

Congratulations to these parents for having the courage to set some limits for their son. In *Ozzie and Harriet Had a Scriptwriter*, David Veerman writes, "Say no to the job; don't allow your teenager to work during the school year." Veerman adds, "However, if your teens want to work during their school vacation weeks and during the summer months, that's a different matter. With no conflicts from school, your teenagers can be encouraged to work as much as possible, saving money for college and the future" (1996: 207-209).

My own philosophy as a youth worker and parent is this: I encourage parents not to have their kids consider a paid job (ten to twenty hours a week) until they're juniors or seniors. I've noticed that, in general, having jobs pushes teens faster into adulthood than is really necessary. They have plenty of years ahead of them to work . Allowing your kids to enjoy their teen years without working lifts a burden off their shoulders and lets them concentrate more on school and church. However, this is just my opinion! You know your teen better than anyone.

# Seasons of Life

*Mark Cannister*

For everything there is a season. Sports seasons, academic seasons, fine arts seasons, weather seasons. Seasons always bring change. There are also many seasons in a teen's life. For example, there are seasons of peer relationships, the first job, spiritual growth, the first date, celebrations (like graduation), the first solo car trip, and so forth. As parents, we need to anticipate these changing seasons and support our children in them. Think of it as outfitting your kids with the proper clothing—the necessary skills—for each season. Just as our kids might welcome a winter coat in December but not in July, a discussion on faith on one day may be meaningless, but on another day it may have profound meaning. Learn to recognize the seasons and the opportunities they present.

# Music and Media

This area should read: PROCEED WITH CAUTION. Music and TV to a teen is like a cup of coffee to an adult. It is his lifeline to reality and the heartbeat to acceptance in the youth culture. How can you intelligently discuss music and media with your kids?

1. Decide to know your teen's music.
You mean listen to Alanis Morissette, Smashing Pumpkins, Madonna, and even Marilyn Manson? Yep! But why? you might be asking. It's simple: You are getting to know your kids by listening to their music. Make sense? Let's go a step further. Read their magazines. Watch the TV shows and videos they view. In his book, *Redeeming Television*, Quentin Schultze calls television "one of the major educators of modern society" (1992, 43).

2. Discuss media together.
When we watch a show or a movie together, I try to make a point to discuss the program's values (or lack thereof). I might ask, "Do you notice how this show portrays Christians as idiots?" "What is this advertisement really saying?" "Is there any truth to this commercial?" Often I will ask our family to explain in their own words what they are watching and hearing. Recently we saw *Evita*. On the way to the theater I challenged my daughter to observe the values of the movie by asking some questions: "Is this truthful?" "Does this message conflict with God's Word?" "What is it saying about happiness?" "What's right and wrong about the rise of Eva Peron?"

My daughter, Rachel, recently wanted to know why I wouldn't let her listen to a particular radio station. I explained, "I am not thrilled with the values the musicians live out. I have some standards that I want to hold to, and I want you to hold to as well. But if you want to tape some of the music, I will listen and discuss the lyrics with you." I guess at that point Rachel decided it was too much work to tape it and listen to it with me! She came back to me about two days later asking me why I wouldn't let her listen to another radio station. I explained that this station airs too many sexual innuendoes. I also had some other concerns:

Dad:     How much time do you think you listen to secular radio in a
          day?
Rachel: I guess about an hour, no, maybe thirty minutes a day.
Dad:     And when do you listen to it?
Rachel: When I'm getting ready for school. I like the commercials and
          news about Hollywood.
Dad:     How about this one? How much time a day do you spend in
          God's Word, just reading by yourself?
Rachel: When do I have time?
Dad:     Well, you watch one TV show a day, so you have the time.
Rachel: Maybe several minutes a week.
Dad:     How about a deal?
Rachel: What?
Dad:     Ever heard the phrase, "Garbage in, garbage out?" What goes in
          will come out. The music you listen to goes into your human
          computer, which stores it all day long. Sometimes the lyrics aren't
          too cool. I have two rules for listening. One: You can listen to this
          station every other day after you have done your homework, but
          not in the morning. Two: You must read at least two passages of
          Scripture a day before you listen to the radio. We will evaluate
          how it's going in a week or so. If you are being consistent, then I
          will allow you the chance to listen to the station on a short-term
          basis. Is that fair?
Rachel: Yeah, that's fair.
Dad:     OK, do we have a deal?
Rachel: Uh-huh, it's a deal.

I encourage all parents to be leaders in this area. And yes, you will need
to reevaluate and keep checking in with how your kids are doing and
what they are listening to and watching.


3. Discern and evaluate.
Ask the question: Should we listen to this music? Should we watch these
shows, videos, and films? There are some shows and movies that I believe
we should not allow our kids to watch. For example, our teenage
daughter is not allowed to watch any R-rated movies for a number of
reasons. One is that it seems most R-rated movies violate biblical
principles. Second, the school she attends asks the students to sign a
contract agreeing that they will not view these movies. Third, my wife
and I do not watch R-rated movies. In other words, we don't say, "Do as I

say, not as I do." We practice what we preach. Set a standard and
follow it.

Extremism gets many families in trouble. We parents should not
go crazy, running into our kids' rooms and smashing their CD players. We cannot constantly try to rescue our children from the media
land mines that are ready to explode. Hiding every TV will not
work. Nor is the opposite extreme the answer either. Letting my kids
watch any shows they want as often as they want is unacceptable.
As a parent, I am unwilling to let the "media monster" run my
child's life. I am not going to let the "boob tube" rock my kids to
sleep each night.


4. Determine structure and guidelines.
Our family rule is simple and clear: No more than one hour of TV
per day. Chores and homework come first. No homework completed, no TV. On Wednesdays as a family we "fast" from TV. It is
off-limits to all. Unlimited usage of media by teenagers is intellectual
and spiritual suicide. This "free-for-all" method compromises our
family's standards and convictions.

Parents who want to be governed by the Spirit of God are called
to imitate God (Ephesians 5:1) and to walk in the light (1 John 1:7).
Bob DeMoss, in his book *Learn to Discern*, suggests that parents set a
family standard concerning the media hype (1992). In other words,
have structure. Monitor the tube. Don't allow your home to be
invaded by trash.

My friend Rick Bundschuh, a youth pastor in Kauai, Hawaii,
urges parents to not "slam" music by saying that rock and roll is of
the devil or that various performers are evil. His rationale?
Statements such as these will trigger the defense mechanism in
every teen to push the limits and eat the forbidden fruit.

Wherever you are in the process, know your guidelines. For married folks, it's imperative that you make a united stand and are on
the same page. You must both be consistent and model to your
teens what is appropriate. Don't hesitate to tell your kids to switch
channels when the junk on TV violates your standards. Homes are
meant to be run by you, not your kids! So be bold and brave. If your
kids hate you for a day, they'll get over it eventually.

# Life or Death

*Mark Cannister*

In the highs and lows of our first pregnancy, my wife and I acquired a new appreciation for the power of an umbilical cord. For the first eight months that cord provided life for our daughter Kelsey, but in the ninth month that same cord became entangled around her neck and she died. The very cord that had given life took away life. There are many things in the routines of teenagers that have the ability to give life and take it away. Relationships, jobs, cars, music, TV, movies, friends, books, school, social activities, and sports can each enhance a teenager's life or destroy it. As parents, we must help our youth to discern when their lives are being enhanced or consumed by the influential factors that they daily encounter.

# All So Different

A couple years ago, one of my teenage daughters, Melissa, toured a local cave during a school outing. At the supper table that evening, she told about the day's experiences.

She conveyed her thoughts and feelings with unusual gusto. In rapid-fire succession she began: "It was all so cool. I mean really cool, about 65 degrees throughout the whole cave! Pools of water, all over the place, containing this unusual species of fish, like, all white. Then bats—everywhere! But the stalactites and stalagmites were the best. They were beautiful! All kinds of sizes and shapes. And the colors! Wow! All so different, yet so neat!"

I will not soon forget Melissa's enthusiastic report.

A new metaphor popped into my head that day: Teens are very much like stalactites and stalagmites.

Some youth develop top-down; for example, they might display their unusual intellectual abilities first. Others mature from the ground up; that is, they might exhibit gifted athletic skills, like running or dancing. They come in all shapes and sizes. Growth spurts fluctuate. Colors vary.

But Melissa put her finger on a great approach to looking at teens. They're "all so different, yet so neat!"

# Knee-High Knowledge

*Doug Randlett*

God blessed my wife, Jane, and me with two undersized boys. No, I really mean it! It was indeed a challenge to encourage their fragile self-images in a macho world. I remember when Mark came home from junior high in a dirty basketball uniform, crying. The problem? The boys on his team rolled him out the door of the bus into a mud puddle. In his hurt and embarrassment he ran home, certain that his size was to blame. Later he found out that the "roll" was a "friend roll." Contrary to his initial thoughts, his teammates really liked him. That lesson was invaluable, as it told him that his physique was for his good and for God's glory.

# ▶ Real Talk ◀

## Love Language

*I always knew that my father loved me, but he seldom said words to that effect. It just wasn't our style to express much emotion. Even when I said good-bye as an adult, I would kiss Mom and shake Dad's hand. But as I stood by the car one day after a vacation visit with my folks, I knew that I had to at least tell Dad how I felt. He was recovering from heart bypass surgery, so it was a poignant moment. I was surprised how difficult it was, but finally, I blurted out, "I love you, Dad" and gave him a hug. He responded, "I love you, too."*

*That was the breakthrough. From that day until his death a few years ago, we made it a practice to say those simple, yet profound words. I wish I could tell him now. I wish I had started sooner.*

*David Veerman*

# Rules of the Game

I grew up in neighborhoods with loads of kids my age. We played baseball, football, dodgeball, and kick-the-can. We made up a bunch of games, too. Sometimes we made up the rules as we went along!

Who makes the rules in your home? Or better yet, what rules make up your home? There are several rules that every family should follow. Here are two guidelines that have particular impact on our communication with teens:

### Rule #1—Include Everyone

Whether it's football, business, or parenting, the game of life is ruined if we do not include others. Since we know that teams (in sports, at the office, or in the home) are built on relationships, all members involved must feel like they are a part of the team's successes. Include those who might be particularly overlooked. Watch out for the younger ones. Ask quieter participants for their ideas. Celebrate together.

### Rule #2—Supercharge Relationships With Genuine Expressions of Love

Often we force youth to comply with our rules (like curfews and dating boundaries). In so doing, we tend to neglect the lifeblood of family relationships—love. We focus too much on the letter of the law, not the spirit.

For instance, one girl told us that she felt included in her family but that she needed more hugs and kisses than she received. How are you communicating unconditional love? What does it sound like in your family? How does it look?

Using rules like these can help you make sure that you are playing fair and communicating love to your teens.

# ACE Up Your Sleeve

*Brian Richardson*

Years ago I discovered A.C.E., a threefold concept that has totally changed how I relate to the teens in my youth groups:

- Adoration: Before entering the youth group room, I stop and say, "These are my kids. God has put them in my charge. I love them. God, help me to show them our love."

- Communication: I make a point to speak to each teen who comes. I try to let each of them know that I'm sincerely interested in what's happening in their lives.

- Evaluation: I keep a 3" x 5" card on each person. I use these cards to make notes about our most recent conversations; to review signs of individual growth and need; to pray for specific requests the kids raise or that I discover; and to remind me to attend as many of their school or community activities as I can.

I've found that parents can take these same three points and use them to build strong relationships with their own teens.

# Truth and Timing

On October 28, 1995, I was flying from Minneapolis, Minnesota, to Regina, Saskatchewan. It happened to be the night of game six in the World Series between the Atlanta Braves and the Cleveland Indians.

A voice came over the cabin speaker, "Ladies and gentlemen, this is your captain speaking. The air traffic controllers in Regina tell us that the Braves are leading one to nothing over the Indians in the bottom of the sixth inning."

Then he added: "I don't know how current that is; we only know what they tell us. We don't have control over the information (what they say) or the time (when they say it)."

That experience got me thinking about teens—especially our responsibility as parents to our own children.

Too often (particularly in early teen years) we are power brokers in our children's lives. We have great influence over both what is taught in the home and when it is taught.

What an awesome responsibility!

As I see it, we can combine the what and the when in four ways. First, we can provide the proper information at an improper time— like telling our kids something important in front of their friends and embarrassing them.

Second, we can offer improper information at the right time. For instance, when a teen who is struggling with a personal loss asks, "Why does God do this to me?" we might unintentionally lie.

Third, we can give the wrong information at the wrong time, like using sarcasm to chastise our kids immediately following some blunder.

Finally, as Christian parents who have access to God's power in Christ, we must regularly remind ourselves of the value of combining truthful information with the most appropriate timing.

After all, that's what we expect from those who lead and teach us. Should our kids expect less from us?

# RELATE

*Brian Richardson*

R  Rationally—Be very intentional about your relationship.

E  Emotionally—Don't be afraid to show your passion and compassion.

L  Loyally—Being fickle strikes the death-blow to any relationship.

A  Authoritatively—Not like some ogre, but as a determined mentor.

T  Tirelessly—Through thick 'n' thin, hang in there.

E  Elastically—Show resiliency and flexibility; power to snap back!

# Sight-Seeing

Three years ago, I visited Washington, D.C. Among other sites, I went with some friends to see the Washington Monument. Two dozen of us rode the vertical lift quickly to the top of this 555-foot obelisk. As we exited, we saw four alcoves providing a view of our nation's capital district to the north, south, east, and west.

When I entered the east alcove, I overheard a conversation between a father and his thirteen-year-old son that went something like this:

Father: Look straight down there, son, and you'll see the U.S. Capitol.

Son: Where?

Father: Right there, where my finger's pointing. See it?

Son: No. Where?

Father: Sitting right in front. You know, it's where the Congress meets. Don't you see it?

Son: Nope!

Father: Hmmm. Let me explain it another way. Way back there, ya see, way back there is RFK Stadium. You know, where the Washington Redskins play football. You see that, don't you?

Son: Oh, sure!

Father: Well, it's directly in front of RFK.

Son: OK, now I see it!

Parents and teens often live in different worlds. In fact, for a parent to be aware of a teen's world is unusual. How are we passing knowledge on to our kids? What are they missing altogether?

Sometimes it's necessary to look at the world through their eyes in order to get our message across. If we aren't willing to change our perspective, our teens may completely miss the view.

# Translation, Please!

*Jana L. Sundene*

"Phat," "da bomb," "tigidy," and "majora." You know what these words mean? No? Well you're not alone! The other day I was at a high school youth meeting and someone asked how many of them were "straight edge." I had a guess—but I didn't want to look out of touch—so I whispered to another adult leader, "Translation, please!" But I've found a better way. Teens like it if I ask them what they mean (though I may get a condescending look). It gives them a chance to explain their world to me. So next time you need a translation, take a deep breath and ask your teen!

# You Make the Call

My father was a referee. And it embarrassed me. At least, as a young teen. Part of the embarrassment stemmed from the fact that, like it or not, referees are always viewed as villains. Let's face it, they typically find themselves in no-win situations. When the final gun or buzzer goes off, you can almost bet on the fact that they've made a new enemy from one team, or the other, or both!

Now, the really weird thing is this: I recently realized that the ref's role in sports parallels the parent's role in the home. Think about it for a second:

- Both start the event.
- Both regulate the play.
- Both interpret the rules.
- Both enforce discipline.
- Both seek fairness and impartiality.
- Both confer with their peers when necessary.
- Both possess basic knowledge and experience.
- Both watch the clock!

Superior referees and superb parents must also "stay on top of their game." Both need to be aware of current changes, such as new jargon or more effective and just rules. They must offer the best possible communication—both what they say and how they say it.

For example, a few years ago, sports announcers coined the phrase, "a good no call." It simply meant that by not calling a penalty for a rule infraction on a given play, the ref made a good call. Confusing, huh?

The same is true in parenting teens—sometimes the best call is no call. The absence of official or parental verbal input does not necessarily signal ignorance or incompetence. Often it means prudence.

So, as legal guardians, let's attempt to be outstanding referees in the home. Even though our calls won't always be appreciated and our interference won't always be valued as being correct, consider the alternative: without proper officials, life's nothing short of chaos.

# Double Jeopardy

*Doug Randlett*

The principle of double jeopardy (not paying for the same crime twice) comes in handy with teens. My wife and I raised both our sons with the understanding that, if they were disciplined outside of our home, the punishment the authority administered was sufficient. And we saw the payoff in our sons' relationship with us and with God. For example, when we as a family regularly shared prayer requests, the boys were honest about any trouble they had been in, knowing that we were not going to punish them again. They were able to open themselves to us and to God. What more could any parent want?

# Respect

In a recent discussion I had with Thom Schultz, founder of Group Publishing, I discovered a secret to disciplining teens I had never heard before. It sounded like it had plenty of potential for all parents.

This nationally known youth leader said that when he speaks to professionals and to parents who love and serve adolescents, he tells them to play a "picture game" when it comes to the difficult subject of discipline.

"In your mind's eye," Thom tells his audience, "pretend that your teen is an adult peer as you discuss issues of necessary discipline." In other words, add about ten or fifteen years to the present age of your teen.

"That way," Thom explains, "you won't be tempted to talk down to your teen. It's tougher to be condescending when you're imagining that you are talking to someone much older. More responsible. To restate it positively, a lot is said about teens honoring their parents. And that's great. That's necessary. But, like trust, respect and honor go both ways. It's mutual. Adolescents need to know that they're intentionally and equally valued in your relationship." Our words (and other communicative patterns) either reflect such respect or not.

Thom added these final thoughts: "And, since discipline is never to be seen as 'punishment' but 'redemption' anyway, it just makes sense to treat youth with the dignity that complements that goal of reconciliation."

So, what approach do you take to this most serious and most troublesome task of disciplining teens? Based upon your kid's reactions to earlier attempts at discipline, how would you rank your attitudes, decisions, communication patterns, and outcomes? How will Thom Schultz's advice help you the next time you have to discipline?

# Truth About Trust

*Doug Randlett*

Scott was one of those kids who struggled with telling the truth. How should Christian parents react to this challenge? One day, my wife Jane and I ignored his childhood pleas during a legitimate illness, thinking it was just another act. It got his attention—big time! God changed his heart and he began a new life. The rule of the house became "Tell the truth and you'll be trusted." Did it work? Scott never had a curfew as a teenager. He was always home when he said he would be, or we got a call of explanation. We were never disappointed about setting a premium on trust. We never regretted our emphasis on the need for mutual responsibility, either.

# Love-and-Logic Parenting

A fascinating book, *Parenting Teens with Love and Logic*, calls teens to responsible living. Authors Foster Cline, M.D., and Jim Fay contend that healthy teenage self-esteem doesn't just happen. It begins when teenagers develop a healthy self-concept through successfully handling responsibility. Parents can bring this about by encouraging teens to find solutions to their own problems. Cline and Fay suggest these thoughts: "It's only natural for parents to want to control their teens. But they must resist their natural urge if they want their teens to mature, and if they want to keep their sanity. . . . The most effective parents are those who thoughtfully surrender control they don't have anyway by offering choices to their teens" (1992, 39).

Cline and Fay call this love-and-logic parenting. It's training teens to grow up; to act responsibly; to make mistakes and then correct them. Love-and-logic parents allow their kids to experience the natural consequences of their mistakes rather than trying to rescue them. The authors cite an example of a coolheaded mom who uses love-and-logic communication methods (Cline and Fay 1992: 166,167).

Mark: OK, if you guys don't love me enough to give me more allowance, I'll just have to start selling drugs!

Mom: Well, I guess that's an option.

Mark: That's an option? What do you mean that's an option?

Mom: (Shrugs) That could be one way to solve your problem.

Mark: You've got to be crazy! What's wrong with you?

Mom: Nothing. Even though I love you more than anything in the world, the time has come when you have to decide for yourself how you are going to live your life.

Mark: No way. You're on something. Otherwise you'd be giving me a lot of grief about this! Do you know that I could get caught for dealing? I could go to jail!

Mom: True. But maybe you'll make enough money dealing that you can hire some good lawyers to get you some light time. I'm sure you've thought it all out. Anyway, just think, if you get caught, the state will take care of you. You won't have to worry about allowance, room and board, or anything.

Mark: Wait a minute! How am I supposed to go to college?

Mom: (Relaxed, reclining on the couch) Oh, you won't be in the slammer forever. With good behavior you'll get out and go to college later. You might even be better prepared because you'll have more life experiences.

Mark: This is weird, man! Are you just going to sit there and let me ruin my life? Don't you even care about what happens to me? I can't listen to this! (Stomps out of the room).

As crazy as this dialogue sounds, it did happen! And the mother's goal was to take the responsibility off her shoulders and put it onto her son's. She did not use manipulation techniques or guilt. She did not lecture or say, "I will not let you talk to me in that manner." She used his statement about drugs and carried it to its logical conclusion. She used his own weaponry, and in response Mark ended up using logic to defend why he shouldn't use drugs!

Love-and-logic parenting is about letting kids own their problems and misfortunes without us parents always bailing them out. It means the teen identifies the problem and searches for a solution.

## Best Father's Day Gift

*Mark H. Senter III*

My Father's Day gift that year wasn't big or expensive. But it was the best. It had been given by my daughter, who had blossomed into a beautiful person. As I looked at my gift, I thought back to the decisions we had made to give our little girl wings. When she was fifteen, we allowed her to travel alone to Aruba so she could gain some experience at a Christian radio station; a year later, we permitted her to drive our conversion van through the construction-clogged expressways of Atlanta; and, on her first date, we told her she could stay out all night at a church-sponsored function. I guess we trusted her ability to make good decisions.

The 3" x 3" cellophane-wrapped plaque read, "Thanks, Dad, for believing in me." Seven years and three offices later, it still hangs at eye level on the wall in front of my desk. Without a doubt it was the best Father's Day gift I have ever received.

# Driving You Crazy

Does your teen sometimes make you feel that you are the only parent in the world who has rules about driving? Do you ever exchange comments such as:

- "I'm the only one of my friends who isn't allowed to drive or stay out late."
- "If you're not careful I won't let you drive until you're 80!"

A study of more than five hundred thousand high school students revealed some common ground among parents of teenage drivers. Ninety-seven percent of these adolescents said they had rules such as telling their parents where they were going in order to use the car. Almost as many teens (95 percent) were not allowed to drink and drive.

Eighty-nine percent were given a curfew, and 81 percent had to tell their folks who they would be with for the evening. Sixty-five percent had to get their parents' permission each time they drove. And if their grades weren't up to par, 47 percent of the kids lost their driving privileges.

My point? Recognize the wisdom of many parents who have gone before you when it comes to primary areas of responsibility, such as driving. Talk it out. Be straight about it. Here is how one father and son talked about drinking and driving (Cline and Fay 1992: 175,176).

Dad: Kyle, if you were to die before you were twenty-one—and I hope you don't—how, statistically, would you die?"
Kyle: I don't know.
Dad: Oh, I bet you do. What are the two major ways teens die?
Kyle: Suicide?
Dad: That's one of them. Do you think you're the suicidal type?
Kyle: No!
Dad: I don't either. So you probably won't die by suicide. How else could you die early?
Kyle: Car accident?
Dad: Right! If you were to die before you were twenty-one, it would probably be in a car accident. And generally in these car accidents, there is something else involved. What is it?
Kyle: Alcohol!
Dad: Right again. Have you ever thought about that before?
Kyle: Not really, I guess.

Dad: I see. Now, think about the kids who die. Do you think that was on their minds the day they were killed?

Kyle: Probably not.

Dad: Kyle, I just want you to know that I love you and would miss you if you were killed before you're twenty-one.

Kyle: I know, Dad. I'll be careful.

Dad: Thanks.

## Judgment Day

*Tim Parsons*

I stood in court with Aaron, a kid who had just received the Lord. Having only known rebellion and selfishness, thoughts of what was right or wrong had never weighed too heavily on his mind before. Today he was faced with a tough decision. Aaron had been caught speeding in a small nearby town. He was summoned to traffic court. Amazingly, the officer who had ticketed him was not present, so everyone before Aaron (each one had been pulled over by the same officer) was pleading not guilty to the judge, with sheepish smiles on their faces. Aaron asked me what he should do but, before I could respond, his turn came. I was so proud when he responded "Guilty, sir!" When the judge asked, "Are you sure?" he replied, "Yes, sir, my walk with God is worth much more than thirty-five dollars."

# Dance Partners for Life

The Grolier Encyclopedia defines dance as "an expression in rhythmic movement of an intensified sense of life."

Sometimes as parents we dance with our kids. But we don't do it to express life—we do it to avoid dealing with life. We dance around issues to avoid conflict because we think conflict will alienate us. Round and round we go without any real closure.

"Do your homework."
"No TV until you _____."
"You're grounded."

How can you become a better dance partner for your child? Don't be afraid to face the music—the real issues of life for your teen.

When your youth says, "I hate my teacher. She's a dork!" Instead of saying, "Don't say that," or "That's not a very Christian thing to say," discover why your kid dislikes her teacher.

Some possible inquiries you could use are:

- Why do you say that?
- What makes you say that?
- Did he say something to you?
- Is there some kind of problem?

Your goal is not to correct initially. Your purpose is to gather information. A lack of communication and information leads to some bad dance moves.

- Step one—skirt the issues
- Step two—ignore their feelings
- Step three—resentment enters
- Step four—discussion closed
- End of dance!

On the other hand, dialogue brings trust, and trust allows us to have deeper, more intimate discussions.

Does that mean that all issues need deep discussion and bridge-building? Not at all. In fact, some issues can be kept to a minimum. Be sensitive to your child's timing and need for talk. Move slowly, with gentleness and a careful step.

# Too Hot to Handle

*Jim Mohler*

As a youth pastor in Phoenix, Arizona, I schedule activities for my youth group throughout the year. However, it gets hot in that desert town—sometimes over 120 degrees! It's not safe to have outside activities at such extreme temperatures. So when the mercury rises, we cancel some events, or move our get-togethers inside or to a cooler time of day.

Sometimes we parents get hot with our teens. Maybe it's us. Maybe it's the subject. Perhaps it's friction between us and our kids. When you feel the heat in your discussions rising, take some time off. Reschedule. You'll find that more can be accomplished when cooler heads prevail.

# Choose Your Battles

Listen to this criticism of teenagers, from somebody who really seems to understand today's kids: "Youth today love luxury. They have bad manners, contempt for authority, no respect for older people, and they talk nonsense—when they should be working" (Rice and Davis 1992).

Do you have any idea who made this statement? It was Socrates, more than five hundred years before Christ!

As someone has rightly concluded: the more things change, the more they stay the same.

But this doesn't diminish our task. To be reminded that adolescent culture—with all its problems—has always been with us doesn't exempt us from parental responsibilities.

Yet as wise parents, we must realize what controversies with our teens are worth fighting for and which ones we need to run away from—those that really don't call for confrontation.

Perhaps the best advice I've heard on this subject came from a sage couple who had raised three teenage boys successfully. They noted that through their many years of parenting, they had reduced their "fights"—the topics that were worth standing up for—to just two areas: morality and eternity.

First, this wise husband-and-wife team said, "Ask yourself if the issue in question addresses a moral concern." Does it break God's laws or human codes? If so, then confrontation is imperative.

Second, the couple queried: "What will your controversy look like, in light of eternity?" To rephrase it, if your conflict will appear quite temporal—or worse, plain silly—in years ahead, it's not worth the battle.

Pick your battles. Life's too short, and we're too finite, to skirmish over every opinion, preference and fad.

# Uzzah's Error

*Duffy Robbins*

The passage in 1 Chronicles 13 shows us a bizarre picture. Uzzah the Israelite is part of a small caravan that is transporting the ark of the covenant. The instructions are quite clear: no one touches the ark. The ark, the symbol of God's presence among the people, must not be profaned by human hands. But the oxen stumble, the ark lurches forward, and instinctively Uzzah reaches out to steady it. It was the last move he made. God struck him dead on the spot.

A curious story to be sure—perhaps one to read to your young children to reinforce that Daddy doesn't want them to touch his new computer! But, maybe the lesson it teaches is more profound than odd. Maybe the lesson we learn from this incident is a reminder to parents that God is in charge. He will steady his own ark. We often shadow the footsteps of our children, anxious for the stumble, fearful of the fall. And yet, we must be warned. It is God who protects our children. It is God—and God alone—who can keep them from falling. And there is a sense in which our amateur attempts become an insult to his sovereignty. All of us want to protect our kids, but there is a fine line between stepping in to give our children a hand and stepping on the sovereign hand of God.

# No Taboos

There was no warning. Not even a hint of what Melissa had on her mind.

"Dad, what does the Bible say about people from different races getting married?"

"What d'ya mean?" I replied, fumbling for a few appropriate words.

"My friend, whose dad is a pastor, says it's wrong. And I was just curious about your thoughts," my sixteen year old answered.

"Well, I don't see anything in the Bible that condemns it," I stated. "Certainly that potential couple would need to give serious consideration to other areas, though, like anticipated prejudice directed against them and any children they might have."

"Yeah, I kinda figured that part out," Melissa interjected.

"But, you know, it's sad to see that many Christians who do have a problem with interracial marriages often don't focus on restrictions that the Bible does have."

"Like what?"

"For starters, like the Scripture being very clear about believers not marrying nonbelievers. Apart from being wrong, it just doesn't work. Values run too deep. Conflicts are inevitable."

"Oh, I know."

"And the many values that are expressed in subjects like Christianity represent the foundation for a bunch of related topics that are often controversial, such as children, money, and leisure time."

"I guess I hadn't thought of it that way," Melissa said. "But that really is true. It's too bad Christians don't concentrate on what's most important."

"Yep, I agree," I concluded, thankful that my daughter felt free enough to discuss such a significant topic in the first place.

I'm certain that part of her motivation to share was based on one of our purposeful household policies: No taboos. In our home, there is no subject that can't be raised for discussion.

It's a simple, yet sometimes risky policy. It requires that we know what we believe (based on the Bible) and how to engage in healthy dialogue. "My way or the highway" attitudes should have no part in our homes.

Do you want your teens to share what's on their minds? Do you desire their confidential thoughts? Make sure they know you're open to discussion—about anything.

# Be Open

*Steve Gerali*

I was asked to speak for a parenting conference on teenagers and sexuality. During this
lecture, I explained in great length the nor-
malcy of having sexual thoughts. This deli-
cate subject still causes a stir in the Christian
community. Because of the sensitivity about
this issue, parents do not talk to their teens
and many teens grow up feeling like they
are either grossly abnormal or defeated
under the guilt of assumed perversion.

At the conference I told parents (fathers
in particular) to let their sons off the hook by
being open to talk about this subject. After
my talk, one man told me he could never
talk to his fourteen-year-old son about this
issue because of how uncomfortable the subject was, yet he didn't want his son to grow
up with the oppression that he felt. The man
asked, "How can I start this conversation
with my kid, so that I can pass on some of
the information that you gave us?"

Starting such a conversation is always
the most difficult thing to do. I told him to
start by finding a safe place to talk. He then
needed to tell his son that this is a hard
topic even for dads to talk about, but that he
wanted to talk about it. I told this man that if
he wanted his son to be open about things
with him, then he had to be open and tell
his son that he also had experienced sexual
thoughts. Creating an intimate, personal,
self-disclosing atmosphere can break the tension that the subject matter may create.

# Laugh

I once heard about a father who placed a sign in his front yard: "For sale, one set of encyclopedias—never used. Teenage son knows everything."

Most teens like humor. I know that my teenage daughter Rachel loves to laugh—even at her own expense. Parents and teens who laugh a lot will have more fun.

Sometimes when it gets tense in our home, I use humor to lighten the situation. Just recently Rachel increased her display of the "rolling eyeball" syndrome. She used to do it a lot when she was around eleven. Back then, I would do my Rodney Dangerfield imitation, rolling my eyeballs back and forth. Since I have big eyes anyway, she would crack up and so would I.

Rolling eyeball syndrome stopped for about a year. Now it's back! Rather than the standard "stop rolling your eyeballs or I will ground you until you are sixteen" spiel, I started using humor to lighten up a little bit.

We were with my parents and sister on Thanksgiving break when Rachel got into one of her teenage moods and started acting up. As we got ready for bed, I said something and Rachel rolled her eyes. Instead of the powerful lecture that I so wanted to deliver, I said to my wife and daughter, "Hey, do you all remember the movie *Dances With Wolves*? Each Indian had a name. I think I will call Rachel 'Rolling Eyes.'" Immediately the tension was gone. Rachel started to smile, then broke into hysterics. Then I said, "And Mommy will be 'Shining Freckles' because of her beautiful freckles and I will be 'Chief Big Nose.'" We cracked up. Sometimes the way to communicate with teens in tense moments is to engage them in humor.

# Cool or Fool?

*David Veerman*

I have seen a Christian musician coax thousands of teens into singing together. This is no easy feat when dealing with high schoolers, who are concerned with their images. How did he do it? He just told the kids, "Don't be too cool to be a fool."

Some people worry so much about being cool—keeping up their image—that they miss out on all the fun in life. Hey, that's good advice for parents too. At times we just need to take a risk, laugh at ourselves, and do something crazy with our family. It'll be fun and it will show our kids that we're real—and cool.

# Never Count Your Chickens

A father noticed that his boy began to keep a box of mementos on his thirteenth birthday. From time to time, he saw his son depositing and withdrawing some curious objects in that box, yet he respected the teen's privacy enough not to disturb him or ask any questions.

One day, sixty months later, as his son was heading out the door on his way to college, the father could no longer check his curiosity.

"Please, tell me what you've been doing with that secret box of yours!" he pleaded.

"Over the years," the young man began, "every time you lectured me or gave me some bad advice, I would simply put an egg in the box."

"Oh," the puzzled parent grunted. "Well, could you show me what's inside, then?"

The contents revealed three eggs, along with fifteen hundred dollars.

"Hey! That's not too bad!" the relieved dad shouted. "Three lousy talks in five years! Great average, huh?"

Then with a second puzzled look, he asked, "How'd you get the fifteen hundred bucks?"

"Oh," the son replied, grinning, "Every time I got twelve eggs, I sold the dozen for two dollars!"

Lectures rarely produce the results we want. Yet we tend to get into the habit of lecturing our teens instead of talking with them.

We can break such poor communication habits by simply doing one thing better: listening before we speak. When we do this, lectures usually become helpful dialogues and bad advice often turns into relevant discussions.

So the next time you're tempted to jump into your preaching mode, remember that there just might be a little box hidden somewhere in your teen's room.

Nobody wins when you lecture. No one benefits. Unless you're selling eggs.

## Seasoned Veteran

*Jim Mohler*

The path of a seasoned veteran necessarily includes many rookie mistakes. In my first year of youth ministry I took a hundred kids on a camping trip a hundred miles away from our church. Halfway home, one of my leaders, an experienced mom, realized that one kid was missing. We left Wayne in San Diego! We were fortunate to find him, and he was OK. But I never left a kid again. In parenting, we may make rookie mistakes that are painful, scary, or even disastrous. It's important to know that we will make mistakes. To become a veteran parent, however, we need to learn from those mistakes. And it doesn't hurt to have a mentor.

# Cheerleading

My wife coaches the middle-school cheerleading squad of which my daughter, Rachel, is the cocaptain. They practice constantly. Cheers, splits, and tumbling routines are regular events at our house. One thing I've come to realize is that all cheerleaders have some things in common:

- They believe in their team and want it to win.
- They want to ignite and maintain the crowd's level of intensity.
- They are out to have a good time and encourage others toward the same goal.
- They are not rude to the other team, coaches, or cheerleaders.

Mom, Dad—you are also cheerleaders. Pull out your verbal pom-poms and cheer for your kids. Use words that inspire. Uplift. Encourage. Motivate. You believe in your kids, so tell them. You want your teens to win, so show them how. Respect, applaud, clap, and leap for your kids. In Proverbs, God says our words are powerful:

- "A man of knowledge uses words with restraint." (17:27)
- "From the fruit of his mouth a man's stomach is filled; with the harvest from his lips he is satisfied." (18:20)
- "The tongue has the power of life and death, and those who love it will eat its fruit."(18:21)
- "He who guards his lips guards his life, but he who speaks rashly will come to ruin." (13:3)
- "The tongue of the wise commends knowledge, but the mouth of the fool gushes folly." (15:2)
- "The tongue that brings healing is a tree of life, but a deceitful tongue crushes the spirit." (15:4)

Watch your words. All good cheerleaders do.

# Encouraging Words

*Steve Gerali*

From the time our daughters could understand language, my wife and I started a habit of telling them four important truths. These were said when we put them to bed at night, when they went to school each morning, whenever they left our house, etc. They are:

1. **Have a great day!**
   We continued to tell our children that this day is a gift from God to be enjoyed and lived in its fullness. God delights when we enjoy the day that he made.

2. **Be the best that you can be today!**
   We never pressured our children to be the absolute best. We reminded them to operate at their fullest potential. This allowed room for failure and growth.

3. **Always remember whose you are!**
   We wanted them to know that they belong to parents who love them. When they entered into a relationship with Christ, we reminded them that they also belong to him. Ownership implies great privilege as well as responsibility.

4. **No matter what, we will love you.**
   Our children know that there is nothing that they can say or do that will ever put them outside of the scope of our love. We reflect our security in God's love and grace when we model this for our children.

# ▶ Real Faith ◀

## Oxygen

*Anytime you fly on a commercial airliner, a flight attendant will instruct you on proper emergency procedures. At some point, he or she will say, "In the event of decreasing cabin pressure, oxygen masks will drop down from the overhead compartment. First, place a mask over your face, and then assist your children." This is not a selfish act. If you cannot breathe, you will be of little use to anyone else. The same is true with our spiritual lives. If we parents are not spiritually strong, then we will not be able to help our children develop their faith. We can never lead our children any further in the faith than we have traveled. So every once in a while, ask yourself if you're first doing what you're asking your teens to do. Personally use the resources at your disposal.*

Mark Cannister

# Let Go

How can we help our children grow up spiritually and build faith? Mark Senter suggests that a three-legged stool can be a symbol for adolescent faith development. The legs are: family, faith community, and designated specialists (at the 2nd International Youth Ministry Congress, 1997). Ron Habermas and I clarified this concept in our book, *Tag-Team Youth Ministry*, which states that teens need spiritual "voices" outside their family systems. Significant others (adults) can serve as mentors, models, and motivators to teens and can complement what parents teach (1995: 13-19, 21-23).

As parents, we must decide if we really want our children to be Christlike. We need to wrestle with a serious question: Will we allow and encourage our kids to be positively influenced by other Christians—both peers and adults? Will we trust adults from local church and parachurch ministries (such as Fellowship of Christian Athletes or Young Life) to invest spiritually in our kids? to speak to their lives? to spend time with our kids? to have them over for dinner? For many parents, this prospect might be quite intimidating.

The church is an extended family of believers. Senter adds that these adults—designated specialists—are not necessarily paid youth pastors, but are men and women who provide support, encouragement, and accountability to teenagers (1997). It is an intergenerational approach to ministry with adolescents. Parent to teen. Adult to teen.

We must view life from a higher level. God wants us to train our kids in the faith. But often we need help. God has provided resources. Our kids will not rise to a new plane of differentiation and experiential faith unless others pour their lives into them. Our kids need mentors to help them grow. So let your child experience the support of family, community, and designated specialists. Let go, and watch your teen stand—on three legs.

# Christ Connections

*Tim Parsons*

I was reminded of the impact of relationships a few weeks ago when I met Eric. This tenth grader was brought by a group of excited friends to a special Sunday morning event at church. The event itself turned out to be mediocre, but Eric accepted Christ as his Savior. His friends were ecstatic! They were so proud of him and of themselves for including him. When the morning was over, they raced to Eric's house to support him as he told his parents the good news. As they neared the house, they saw several cars and lots of commotion. They entered the house to find that, while Eric was at church, his mother had died. Quickly they surrounded him with love and supportive hugs. Although devastated, Eric was immediately blended into our group and he remains with us still. He met the One he needed on the very day he needed him the most! And close friends helped him make that eternal connection—a connection that also provided so much for him in this life, as well. What healing connections do your teens have?

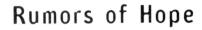

# Rumors of Hope

Sociologist Peter L. Berger told the story of a priest who worked in a European slum. Asked why he was committed to this type of work, the man responded: "So that the rumor of God may not disappear completely" (1969: 94,95).

As parents of teens, we are obligated to start "rumors" and keep them alive. That is, in the midst of a society that often acts as the foe of the family, we must advance a special hope. We have the duty to communicate that, in Christ, we can have real security. We must pass on the rumor that life and reality are bigger than what the world shows us.

How do we advance this hope? Let me suggest two ways that we pass on rumors.

First, we communicate explicitly. We must take advantage of moments to teach our teens about the hope that Jesus provides. We need to teach relevant truths like the assurance of our salvation, how to pray and read the Bible, how to get along with others, how to determine God's will for us, and how to have peace in a restless world.

Second and more importantly, we also need to pass on rumors of our faith's security by implicit communication. We do this by our attitudes, behaviors, and moods rather than our words.

Specifically, I believe that we parents speak this language best with humor and honesty. I've found that if there's one thing that strongly connects me with my kids, it's humor. Simply put, have fun with them. Laugh, joke, and smile until the corners of your mouth touch each ear. (Caution: Don't use your youth as the butt of your jokes. Steer clear of sarcasm directed at them.) Enjoy your kids. From time to time, laugh at yourself as well.

Also, remember that "honesty is the best policy" when it comes to rumor talk. If you want your teens to catch the hope you have in Jesus, be honest. Life is tough, even for those who know Christ. Be sure your kids see in you how to wrestle with life when the bottom falls out. Be sure they get both the message of your sincerity and your guidelines for survival in difficult times.

One last thing. Like it or not, your teen will hear rumors from your life and conversations. You choose whether they will hear rumors of security and hope, or just the opposite.

# Apologies Accepted

*David Veerman*

Perhaps the most difficult words to say are "I was wrong. Will you forgive me?" People in general find it tough to apologize because doing so admits weakness. And no one wants to appear weak. We parents especially find it hard to apologize to our children. I suppose that's because we like to be in control, to have all the answers. Yet our kids need to know that we're human, that we make mistakes, and that there's life after failure. If you've blown it, be quick to admit it and say, "I'm sorry." Yes, they're tough words to say, but they also express genuine love.

# Three Rs of Faith-Building Communication

"What's brown, furry, has four legs, and a tail?" queried Mrs. Howard of her fourth-grade Sunday school class.

Silence, although several children shot glances of confusion at each other.

"Oh, come on!" the teacher prodded. "You know what I'm referring to! It lives in trees and it gathers nuts for the winter."

Susie, often the spokesperson for the class, took a chance. "Well, Mrs. Howard, it sounds like you're describing a squirrel," she began, scrutinizing her classmates' faces for some measure of support. "But to be on the safe side, I'll say the answer is Jesus!"

Unfortunately, too many churches' question-and-answer times sound just like this. Instruction for teenagers and adults alike often includes similar no-brainers.

But such instruction is not limited to the church. The Christian home must also shoulder its fair share of blame for not properly stimulating youth to grow in their faith.

As parents, it's crucial for us to use our conversations for teens to grow. To this end, consider the "Three Rs" of faith-building communication between parents and teens.

### Reverent

Parents must be students of Scripture if they want their kids to honor the Lord. You can bet that most teens can quickly and accurately state whether or not their dads and moms love and obey the Bible. How do we show respect for areas of our faith we say are important to us?

### Relevant

As spiritual caregivers, we should be sensitive to our teens' culture in order to know how to make the Word meaningful to them without compromising it. This includes the need for parents actively to study their surroundings, asking how they live out their faith in today's society.

### Reflective

One of the best metaphors of the Christian life is a pilgrimage. Through reflective discussions and the purposeful recall of our life experiences, we regularly seek to align ourselves with God's purposes. We must also be willing to raise tough questions about life and faith with our teens; for example, to wrestle with classic issues such as, "Why do bad things happen to good people?"

Faithful practice of these "Three Rs" tends to produce faithful believers of all ages.

## Excellent Example

*Matt Wilmington*

How could young Joseph resist the sexual temptation of Potiphar's wife? One possibility is that he respected God's holiness, a respect that may have been nurtured, in part, because of his father's example. Now, Jacob was not exactly a perfect father, but he did respect God's holiness. When Joseph was a boy, Jacob led his family in a radical revival (see Genesis 35:1-7). They threw out their idols, purified themselves, and changed their clothes. Catch the symbolism? Jacob wanted to deliver his family from their habits, routine sins, and cultural snares. What an example to Joseph!

As an adolescent, I became aware of the moral failure of two respected pastors. In my confusion and spiritual frustration, I demanded an answer from my father. He humbly replied, "Others have committed adultery, but I haven't!" Yes, my father taught me to keep my eyes on Christ. But his powerful real-life model of respect for God's holiness didn't hurt either.

# Tradition

The message of *Fiddler on the Roof*, the long-running Broadway hit, identifies the fundamental challenge within contemporary Christian homes: What happens when traditions encounter modern-day calls for change?

In the play, a poor Jewish milkman, Tevye, tries to marry off his three oldest daughters. But each daughter chooses a husband in spite of her father's wishes. Each successive marriage ceremony strays further and further from Jewish tradition. During the opening monologue, Tevye explains the symbolism of the play's title: "A fiddler on the roof. Sounds crazy, no? But here, in our village of Anatevka, you might say every one of us is a fiddler on the roof, trying to scratch out a pleasant, simple tune without breaking his neck. It isn't easy."

Parents of Christian households empathize with the fiddler metaphor. Hostility toward traditional patterns of caregiving increases daily, complicating the goal "to scratch out a pleasant, simple" lifestyle. Leaders of these households don't need more opposition. But resistance comes nevertheless. Challenges to totally revamp, or even destroy, foundational practices of Christian faith in the home continue. Value systems topple. Pressures of both single-parent and blended families affect every member of the home.

Although its story is set in czarist Russia a hundred years ago, *Fiddler's* message is as relevant as today's evening news, for Tevye continues his analogy of the fiddler: "You may ask, Why do we stay up there if it's so dangerous? Well, we stay because Anatevka is our home. And how do we keep our balance? That, I can tell you in one word: tradition!" Then, as the popular opening song ("Tradition") begins, Tevye declares, "We have traditions for everything. How to sleep. How to eat. How to work. How to wear clothes."

Suddenly, the tiniest crack in this father's Judaic traditions appears. Following his illustrations of how their multiple customs reflect continuous devotion to God, Tevye says: "You may ask, How did this tradition get started?" Then he surprises himself by his own answer: "I'll tell . . . I don't know!" He concludes, "But it's a tradition. And, because of our traditions, every one of us knows who he is and what God expects him to do."

Contemporary Christian parents share this dilemma with Tevye; many retain confidence in very traditional beliefs yet, when pressed, are ignorant of basic faith tenets. If Christian parents are to be effective with their kids—and with their teens, in particular—they will consistently have to explain both the what and the why of their faith in their conversations. The what is the content that we share; the why is the rationale.

Traditions crumble when either element is missing. They become hollow. If we are serious about Christian values, let's be sure to do our homework for our teens. Let's have conversations that offer the "reason for the hope," as Peter challenges us in 1 Peter 3:15 (Habermas 1994: 280-295).

## More Than Memorizing

*David Veerman*

When our two daughters were quite young, we memorized verses as a family. One evening Gail and I heard the girls arguing in their bedroom. "I hate you!" one screamed. The other responded in kind (actually in "unkind"). Instead of running to intervene, I called out, "Kara?"

It got quiet, and she replied, "Yes?"

"What's our Bible verse for this week?"

Very sweetly she replied, in perfect form, "First John 4:11 (TLB): 'Dear friends, since God loved us as much as that, we surely ought to love each other too." Then, with barely a pause, the fight resumed with all its intensity. Kara had learned the words, but she missed their meaning and application. She failed to let Scripture change her behavior. Unfortunately, most believers—parents included—make the same mistake. Certainly we should teach God's Word to our kids. But as they approach their teen years, we need to help them implement and live what they've learned.

# Power of Prayer

Fascinating results from a recent poll of one thousand adults in the U.S. (conducted in February, 1996) have the medical field buzzing. It should greatly encourage parents of adolescents, as well.

The poll showed that 79 percent believed that "spiritual faith can help people recover from illness, injury, or disease." Other research supports this poll. For example, two 1994 National Institute of Mental Health studies (of more than 2,500 patients each) found that frequent churchgoers and those who prayed had fewer bouts of depression and other mental illnesses. It also showed that they had significantly lower rates of alcohol and drug abuse (McNichol 1997).

What does this survey say to parents? A lot! Faith does matter, even when it comes to physical well-being. Prayer changes things. Families who are serious about their religious beliefs tend to be healthier in body, mind, and spirit.

You know your kids are watching you. How clear and consistent is your personal example of spiritual health to your youth? For example, what's the nature of your prayer life on their behalf? What do your daily habits say about taking care of your body? To modify a well-known saying: The family that prays together, stays together—much, much longer!

# Actions Speak

*Jana L. Sundene*

I'm one of those lucky people who can eat anything and not gain weight. I never worried about eating well-balanced, nutritional meals until one day at a fast-food restaurant. I noticed two overweight girls from my youth group watching me as I dipped my fries into my hot fudge sundae. (Yes, you heard me!) It was natural for them to watch me. I was their youth leader. I felt a wave of guilt and concern as I remembered that teens don't get inspired by what we say, but by what we do. That's how teens learn how to be adults. If your adolescent isn't responding to your words, look at what your actions might be telling them. You could be sending totally different messages.

# A Creative Approach

Recently I asked a friend how she mastered computers. "Trial and error," she stated. "I kept experimenting until I got it right." Pretty good advice, but I wasn't satisfied. "How did you know what to do?" She replied, "I read the manual."

Let me suggest something practical and simple: Read God's manual, the Bible. It has marvelous advice and is remarkably realistic. It's inspired by God, you know.

There are many things the Bible tells us to do for our children. Love them. Teach them truth. Model godliness to them. Forgive them. Communicate with them. Pray for them. But God also gives us the responsibility of choosing how to communicate his truth. At times we need to experiment as we implement biblical principles. It does take some creativity. Here are a few ideas you may want to try.

1. Write it down.
Several years ago, I spoke at a church about making memories for our kids. One father there gave me a great idea. Following the service, he told me that when many memories and stories of his first child started to fade, he began to write a "book" for her. He would write stories about her, pieces of advice, and pearls of wisdom. He compiled his thoughts in a journal and gave it to her as a graduation present. What a gift!

I liked his idea so much that I started a journal too! Boy, has it been fun remembering and looking ahead. Perhaps this could be a good experiment for you. You might consider entering a few thoughts on the computer each week, or writing some ideas in a notebook several times a month. It could be a treasure of illustrations that will last a lifetime.

2. Camp out.
One couple didn't know how to talk about sexuality with their two children. They read books by the experts but still felt inadequate. One weekend they took their teens camping in the mountains. Each night, both parents shared what was in their hearts. "We're really scared for you and your friends. So many teens are not prepared to deal with the opposite sex. How do you feel about kissing? Making out? Petting? Intercourse?"

This family spent many hours drinking hot chocolate and talking about the real stuff of life. It was an experiment that brought openness to their family. Several years later when the kids were tempted, they knew they could talk to their parents about sexuality.

Build some memories. A Yiddish proverb says, "If you want to be successful, do three things. Have a child, plant a tree, and write a book." Why these three? Because they will live on when you are gone.

Since you've had children, and probably planted a tree, why not write a book? A book to your kids. Or take them for a weekend hike and make some stories to remember!

## Why Wait?

*Matt Wilmington*

Here's a creative approach to answer this question from your teens. Consider the following conversation of a teenage couple as they sat on a hill overlooking their small town.

"I don't know about you, but sexual pressure feels even stronger as we get closer to our marriage," she confessed.

"Tell me about it! Guys at the shop talk like it's just the natural thing to do if we truly love each other," he added.

"It seems like it's the accepted thing. But we've got to be careful. Our relationship is special. I don't want to mess it up," she insisted.

"What if you would get pregnant? It would devastate our parents," he said. "But it's still hard to wait!"

"We both know that God knows best, and he wants us to wait. Maybe—just maybe—he's got some incredible plans for our future," she sighed.

"Always the dreamer," he teased. "Gotta go. See you tomorrow."

"Good night, Joseph. I love you."

"Sweet dreams, Mary. I love you, too."

# Legacies

Why does Ecclesiastes 7:1 affirm that "the day of death" is "better than the day of birth"? How can Solomon write this? What could be more exciting and invigorating than a new life with limitless possibilities? How can one's last breath be better than the first? I think Solomon is talking about legacies.

I've attended a number of funerals. I've learned that a person's death can describe his life. While the organ plays at the funeral home and the minister speaks about the deceased, an entire life story is told and retold to many. The minister recalls, "Michael was a caring father. A loving husband. A man of deep faith and integrity."

Eulogies often reveal the legacies, the lasting impressions a man or woman leaves others. The Bible speaks of the sins of the father being passed down to the third and fourth generations. It also says that love and obedience can be reproduced from generation to generation. Legacies.

What do you want your kids to say about you at your funeral? "No one has power over the day of his death" states Ecclesiastes 8:8. We have no leverage, power, or authority over death. But we do over our daily lives. We can make wise decisions each day. We can effectively serve God each day. We can love our families every day.

Ask yourself two vital questions. First, how do you want to live your life with meaning and purpose? And second, what kind of legacy do you want to pass down to your children?

Let's start with the first question. When I was eighteen, I came to Christ. Before that time, I had lived selfishly. I was a drug user and pusher in high school. I had been arrested for marijuana possession twice. As I started to grow in Christ, I had to decide whether I would continue my sinful lifestyle of drinking, smoking, and drug abuse. I read in John 10:10 that Jesus said, "I have come that they may have life, and have it to the full." I chose to live my life for God. That meant changing my way of thinking. I altered my values and priorities to reflect the kingdom of God, not the kingdom of self. It's taken twenty-three years, but my mission has changed from being selfish to loving God, my wife and children, and to making disciples for Jesus Christ.

How do you answer the second question: What kind of legacy do you want to pass down to your children? As a follower of Jesus, I want my life to reflect his life. I want to model Christlike love, forgiveness, humor, prayer, generosity, and compassion, especially to my family. I'm not just interested in my kids enjoying basketball or chocolate cookies because I do. I want to pass on eternal values. And when my family, coworkers, and friends arrive at my funeral, I hope I will have inspired them to want to live forever with the Lord Jesus. May each of us know that the day of our death is better than our birth, due to the fact that we have lived life each day to the fullest for the glory of God and we will be welcomed into our eternal home.

## Marathon Model

*David Veerman*

I have completed five marathon races of 26.2 grueling miles each. Each race is unique, but all races are similar too. I found direct parallels to life. As a young man, I thought of life as a sprint—go fast, run hard, reach the goal as quickly as possible, win the prize. But I have learned that a marathon provides a much more accurate picture: prepare, train, set the right pace, fight through pain, work with others, use your head, keep your eyes on the goal, show perseverance and patience. Finally, at some point in the future, we will be able to say, "I have finished the course; I have kept the faith."

# About the Authors

Ron Habermas is the McGee Professor of Biblical Studies at John Brown University in Siloam Springs, Arkansas. He speaks frequently around the country and is the author of five books including *Teaching for Reconciliation*, which he coauthored with Klaus Issler. Ron and Mary, his wife of twenty-five years, have three children: Elizabeth (age 20), Melissa (age 16), and Susan (age 12).

David Olshine is the Chair of Youth Ministries at Columbia International University in Columbia, South Carolina. He has authored a number of books, including *Staying on Top: Creative Study of Philippians* and *Actual Reality* (creative study on 1 John, coauthored with Helen Musick). For the past nineteen years, David has been actively involved in youth ministry. He speaks to thousands of youth, youth workers, and parents of teens annually. David and his wife, Rhonda, are the parents of one teenager, Rachel (14).

David and Ron have coauthored two other books with Standard, *Down But Not Out Parenting* and *Tag-Team Youth Ministry*.

# About the Guest Authors

Mark Cannister is Assistant Professor of Youth Ministries and the Chair of the Youth Ministries Program, Division of the Humanities, Gordon College, Wenham, Massachusetts.

Steve Gerali is an author, lecturer, and Chair of the Department of Youth Ministry and Adolescent Studies at Judson College in Elgin, Illinois.

James W. Mohler is Chairman of the Youth Ministries Department of the College of Arts and Sciences, Trinity International University, Deerfield, Illinois.

Les Parrott is a Professor of Psychology at Seattle Pacific University, Seattle, Washington. He has authored several books including *Helping the Struggling Adolescent*.

Tim Parsons is a Professor of Youth Ministry at Lexington Baptist College, Lexington, Kentucky.

Douglas H. Randlett is Chairman of the Department of Church Ministries, Missions, and Cross-Cultural Studies; and Associate Professor of Church and Youth Ministries at the Center for Youth Ministry, Liberty University, Lynchburg, Virginia.

Bryan Richardson is the Basil Manly, Jr., Professor of Christian Education at Southern Baptist Theological Seminary, Louisville, Kentucky.

Duffy Robbins is the Chairman and Associate Professor of Youth Ministries at Eastern College, St. Davids, Pennsylvania. He is the coauthor of *Spontaneous Melodramas* and *Memory Makers*.

Mark Senter III is the Vice President and Dean of the Division of Open Studies at Trinity International University, Deerfield, Illinois, and coeditor of *Reaching a Generation for Christ*.

Jana Sundene is a Professor of Youth Ministry at Trinity International University, Deerfield, Illinois.

Dave Veerman, author of *Ozzie and Harriet Had a Scriptwriter,* is a partner in the Livingstone Corporation, Naperville, Illinois.

Matthew L. Wilmington is Assistant Professor of Youth Ministries at the Center for Youth Ministry, Liberty University, Lynchburg, VA.

# Works Cited

Benson, Peter L. *The Quicksilver Years*. San Francisco: Harper and Row, 1987.

Berger, Peter L. *A Rumor of Angels*. Garden City: Archer Books, 1969.

Berman, Bill, and Dale Doty. *Shaking the Family Tree*. Wheaton: Victor Books, 1991.

Cline, Foster, M.D., and Jim Fay. *Parenting Teens With Love and Logic*. Colorado Springs: Pinon Press, 1992.

Curran, Dolores. *Traits of a Healthy Family*. Minneapolis: Winston Press, 1983.

Habermas, Ron. "The Family as a Context for Spiritual Formation." In *The Christian Educator's Handbook on Spiritual Formation*, edited by K. O. Gangel and J. C. Wilhot. Wheaton: Victor Books, 1994.

Habermas, Ron, and David Olshine. *Tag-Team Youth Ministry*. Cincinnati: Standard Publishing, 1995.

Kesler, Jay. *Ten Mistakes Parents Make With Teenagers (and How to Avoid Them)*. Brentwood: Wolgemuth & Hyatt Publishers, 1988.

McGinnis, Alan Loy. *The Friendship Factor*. Minneapolis: Augsburg, 1979.

McNichol, Tom. "The New Faith in Medicine." *USA Weekend* (April 1997): 34.

Narramore, Bruce. *Adolescence Is Not an Illness*. Old Tappan: Fleming Revell, 1980.

Olshine, David. "Scanning Beneath The Surface: A Look At Family Systems." *Youthworker* (May/June 1996): 34.

Olshine, David, and Ron Habermas. *Down But Not Out Parenting.* Cincinnati: Standard Publishing, 1995.

Rice, Wayne, and Ken Davis. *Understanding Your Teenager.* Youth Specialties/Zondervan, 1992. Video.

Schultz, Quentin. *Redeeming Television.* Downers Grove: Intervarsity, 1992.

Senter III, Mark. At the 2nd International Youth Ministry Congress. Oxford, 1997.

Shirey, John. "Hands-on Parenting Works For Us." *Fantastic Flyer.* Atlanta: Two Roads Publishing, 1997.

Smith, Tim. *The Relaxed Parent.* Chicago: Northfield Publishing, 1996.

*USA Today.* January 16, 1997.

Veerman, David. *Ozzie and Harriet Had a Scriptwriter.* Wheaton: Tyndale House, 1996.

Wright, Norm. *The Power of a Parent's Words.* Ventura: Regal, 1991.

# Parenting Resources

## Books

Brown, Joseph, and Dana Christensen. *Family Therapy Theory and Practice.* Monterey: Brooks/Cole, 1986.

Cline, Foster, M.D., and Fay, Jim. *Parenting Teens With Love and Logic.* Colorado Springs: Pinon Press, 1992.

Cloud, Henry, and John Townsend. *Boundaries.* Grand Rapids: Zondervan, 1992.

DeMoss, Bob. *Learn to Discern.* Grand Rapids: Zondervan, 1992.

Friedman, Edwin. *Generation to Generation.* New York: Guildford, 1985.

Habermas, Ron, and David Olshine. *Tag-Team Youth Ministry.* Cincinnati: Standard Publishing, 1995.

Huggins, Kevin. *Parenting Adolescents.* Colorado Springs: NavPress, 1990.

Kesler, Jay. *Ten Mistakes Parents Make With Teenagers (And How To Avoid Them).* Brentwood: Wolgemuth & Hyatt, 1988.

Leman, Kevin. *Bringing Up Kids Without Tearing Them Down.* New York: Delacorte Press, 1993.

McGoldrick, Monica, and Randy Gerson. *Genograms in Family Assessment.* New York: Norton Press, 1985.

Medved, Michael. *Hollywood Vs. America.* New York: Harper Collins, 1992.

Menconi, Al. *Staying in Tune: A Sane Response to Your Child's Music.* Cincinnati: Standard Publishing, 1996.

Mueller, Walt. *Understanding Today's Youth Culture*. Wheaton: Tyndale House, 1994.

Olshine, David, and Ron Habermas. *Down But Not Out Parenting*. Cincinnati: Standard Publishing, 1995.

Parrott, Les. *Helping the Struggling Adolescent*. Grand Rapids: Zondervan, 1992.

Schultze, Quentin. *Dancing in the Dark*. Grand Rapids: Eerdmans, 1991.

Smith, Tim. *The Relaxed Parent*. Chicago: Northfield Publishing, 1996.

Veerman, David. *Ozzie and Harriet Had a Scriptwriter*. Wheaton: Tyndale House, 1996.

## Videos

Edge TV, P. O. Box 35005, Colorado Springs, CO 80935-9936 (800) 616-EDGE.

Garrett, Dan. Home Team Video. P. O. Box 82, West Point, GA 31833.

Rice, Wayne and Ken Davis. *Understanding Your Teenager*. Youth Specialties/Zondervan, 1992. (619) 440-2333 or (800) 776-8008.